THE NON-PROPHET'S GUIDE™ TO HEAVEN

Written & Illustrated by
TODD HAMPSON

HARVEST PROPHECY
AN IMPRINT OF HARVEST HOUSE PUBLISHERS

Published in association with William K. Jensen Literary Agency, 119 Bampton Court, Eugene, Oregon 97404.

Cover design by Bryce Williamson

Cover illustration © Todd Hampson

Interior design by Chad Dougherty

THE NON-PROPHET'S GUIDE is a trademark of The Hawkins Children's LLC. Harvest House Publishers, Inc., is the exclusive licensee of the trademark THE NON-PROPHET'S GUIDE.

For bulk, special sales, or ministry purchases, please call 1-800-547-8979.
Email: CustomerService@hhpbooks.com

This logo is a federally registered trademark of the Hawkins Children's LLC. Harvest House Publishers, Inc., is the exclusive licensee of this trademark.

The Non-Prophet's Guide™ to Heaven
Copyright © 2024—Text © Todd Hampson. Artwork © Todd Hampson
Published by Harvest House Publishers
Eugene, Oregon 97408
www.harvesthousepublishers.com

ISBN 978-0-7369-8638-0 (pbk)
ISBN 978-0-7369-8639-7 (eBook)

Library of Congress Control Number: 2024931182

Printed in the United States of America

24 25 26 27 28 29 30 31 32 / VP / 10 9 8 7 6 5 4 3 2 1

Dedicated to our daughter Natalie—"God's Girl."
His sovereign touch has been on your life since long before that wonderful
Christmas morning when you were born. Your mom and I are so proud of the
woman you have become. As you pursue your calling and the adventures the
Lord has in store, never forget that you will always be our "Baby Girl."

Psalm 139:13-18

CONTENTS

SECTION 4: Secondary Questions About Heaven

SECTION 5: What Difference Does Heaven Make Now?

INTRODUCTION

Heavenly Minded and Earthly Good

*Set your minds on the things that are above,
not on the things that are on earth.*

COLOSSIANS 3:2 NASB

We sat on the edge of a rocky creek, our clothes still wet from flipping over rocks searching for crayfish and "accidentally" falling completely into the cool mountain stream. The summer sun warmed our backs as the soothing sounds of the winding water became the soundtrack for the story we were about to hear. The rugged log that served as our pew became saturated as our clothes dripped while we awaited our camp counselor's Bible devotion to begin.

I—along with eight or nine others in our group—wanted to keep playing in the creek. But it was time for another "boring" Bible lesson, or so I thought. Our cabin leader, Doug, a dad in his early forties, sacrificed a few weeks each summer to brave the noble and dangerous calling of leading groups of the unruly organisms, known as middle-school boys, outside in the beauty of God's creation.

After some introductory remarks and camp instructions—including many reminders to quiet down and listen—Doug began to describe the experience of jumping out of an airplane and landing safely on the ground via the use of a parachute. For around ten minutes, he methodically described the tedious preparation of all the details that had to take place in order to jump from a moving plane in the sky. A full-body jumpsuit had to be meticulously donned. Boots had to be laced up and tied correctly. The parachute had to be precisely folded and packed. The plane had to be fueled up, and go through a rigorous and time-consuming safety check. Each jumper had to have their harnesses checked and double-checked. Also, the weather had to cooperate before they could receive the green light to fly.

By the time Doug finished explaining all the preparatory details, we felt somewhat exhausted just listening. All of that, just to jump out of a plane with a parachute? It sounded like a lot of work to simply abandon a perfectly good aircraft. But then he unpacked details of the jump itself. He described the nervous anticipation he felt as the plane took off. He talked about how, when the correct altitude was reached, the jump door was opened and the reality of what was about to take place set in. Things got very real, very quickly. His knees knocked. His stomach churned. His adrenaline surged and his pupils dilated. Our gifted storyteller described the moment when he crossed the threshold and jumped out into thin air—placing his trust and his life into a piece of cloth and a harness.

With great detail and passion, Doug described what he saw from such a high altitude as he flew through the air. He explained the exhilarating feeling of adventure he felt as he hurtled toward the earth. He told us about the moment the chute opened and he was suddenly yanked to a slower speed. Doug shared how he could feel his heart pounding in his chest with excitement as that occurred and how he paused to look around—supposed to be able to see for a hundred miles in each direction. He shared that as soon as he landed, he couldn't wait to go up again, and how experiences like this defy description.

We were riveted by his story as our imaginations placed us in his boots. We saw ourselves jumping out of that plane. We could almost feel the wind hitting our faces and sense the yank on our bodies the moment the parachute opened. Our earlier chatter had become silence. Our camp counselor had us right where he wanted us, filled with rapt attention and ready to hear how this story connected with the Bible.

Our leader pivoted, and he shared a few verses about heaven and how different our bodies will be when we are there. He described how we could skip the tedious task of putting on the jump suit, lacing up the boots, packing a parachute, wearing the uncomfortable harness, or needing a safety check. In fact, we wouldn't even need a plane! Our riveting storyteller effectively shifted our mind's eye from earthly things to the reality of heaven— as much as the minds of unchurched, pre-Christian, middle-school-aged boys could.

Though I was not yet a believer in Christ, heaven drew me. At the core of my being, I knew there was more to life than what we see. Eternity is in the heart of man (Ecclesiastes 3:11)—and middle-school boys. Everyone—from the firm agnostic, to the devout believer, to the pantheistic unreached tribal group member—has some concept of eternity.

Even staunch naturalists—when pushed—have to admit that something is eternal. If there was ever a time when nothing existed, nothing could exist now because something can't come from nothing. Therefore, the naturalist posits that the universe itself is eternal—cycling through an endless rubber band of explosion, expansion, energy loss, and contraction. Rinse and repeat ad nauseam. They propose that a singularity (all matter condensed to a tiny speck) explodes, expands, and contracts over and over again.

But even within the naturalist's explanation of the universe, there are major foundational problems with their thesis. Where did the matter originally come from? What caused the first explosion? What guides the forces that affect matter, space, and time? What controls heat, gravity, energy, and inertia? The pure naturalist has no valid or reasonable explanation. Even for the staunch naturalist, logic dictates a supernatural and eternal conclusion to the question of origins. I'm not even talking about biological origins. I mean the origins of anything and everything that exists. No matter how you slice it, logic and fact demand some kind of supernatural beginning to the space-time continuum.

The Non-Prophet's Guide to Heaven

As human beings, we know this intuitively. That's why remote tribes offer sacrifices to appease their "gods." That is why atheists rail so hard against those of us who believe in God and the supernatural. They reject the notion of God and are angry with him simultaneously. King Solomon states it simply in Ecclesiastes 3:11. To paraphrase, God has placed eternity in the heart of humankind. It is imprinted. It is part of us. It is an essential piece of what it means to be human—created in the image of God.

Think about it for a moment. Animals don't think about eternity past or eternity future. My family has two dogs, and I did an experiment. I asked the dogs if they wanted 100 pounds of doggie treats tomorrow or a single doggie treat today. I explained it very carefully. Then I set the single treats before them and gave them the opportunity to make their choice, one treat now or 100 pounds of treats the next day.

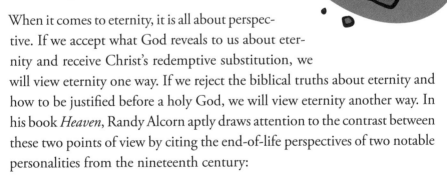

They instantly chose now. Obviously I'm joking here, but you get the picture. Animals are a different type of being. They may have a personality, talents, instincts, and emotions, but I guarantee they never contemplate the things that humans do as God's image-bearers.

When it comes to eternity, it is all about perspective. If we accept what God reveals to us about eternity and receive Christ's redemptive substitution, we will view eternity one way. If we reject the biblical truths about eternity and how to be justified before a holy God, we will view eternity another way. In his book *Heaven*, Randy Alcorn aptly draws attention to the contrast between these two points of view by citing the end-of-life perspectives of two notable personalities from the nineteenth century:

> When it came to Heaven and Hell, Mark Twain never quite got it. Under the weight of age, he said in his autobiography, "The burden of pain, care, misery grows heavier year by year. At length

ambition is dead, pride is dead, vanity is dead, longing for release is in their place. It comes at last—the only unpoisoned gift earth ever had for them—and they vanish from a world where they were of no consequence; where they achieved nothing; where they were a mistake and a failure and a foolishness."

What a contrast to the perspective that Charles Spurgeon, his contemporary, had on death: "To come to Thee is to come home from exile, to come to land out of the raging storm, to come to rest after long labour, to come to the goal of my desires and the summit of my wishes."[1]

MARK TWAIN   CHARLES SPURGEON

What About Near-Death Experiences?

There has been a plethora of books, TV shows, and movies about near-death experiences, trips to heaven, trips to hell, and everything in between. Many of these stories tug at the heart strings and seem like they could be credible accounts made by honest people. Yet, they often contain conflicting information between retellings. Worse yet, the details that are given are often at odds with clear information given to us in God's Word—the Bible.

So, how do we reason through these stories, conflicting accounts, and widely varying details about the afterlife? Simple. We turn to *the* source of Truth. The Bible is our plumb line. Using modern-day construction terms, it is our level. It is the single standard by which we evaluate all accounts.

I'll say it plainly (and I'll make my case throughout this book): If anything you hear does not square with the clear truth of Scripture, throw it out. Time and eternity will prove it false. We may not know everything about heaven, but the Bible does provide us with what we need to know about it. When it comes to wild speculation, we need to remember the principle given in Deuteronomy 29:29, which reads, "The secret things belong to the LORD our God, but the things *revealed* belong to us and to our children forever, that we may follow all the words of this law." We can bank on what God *has* revealed, and we can confidently reject anything that contradicts his Word.

That being said, I have personally known believers who were present at the time of a loved one's passing. And in many cases, as their loved one neared death, they gave witness to seeing a glimpse of heaven or even the Savior. Or, after days of unconsciousness, they opened their eyes wide and began to talk about seeing Jesus and loved ones who had gone before. I won't share the names or personal stories of others without permission, but these are level-headed, nonsensational people of integrity. Best of all, their accounts ring true, align with Scripture, and provide great comfort and hope.

Practically There

The title of this opening chapter reminds us that if we are truly heavenly minded, we will be earthly good. Without a doubt, there are believers who know their Bible well but don't live out their Bible well. They *learn* theology but they don't *do* theology. They fill their head with Bible knowledge but fail to activate it. Because of this tendency in some modern church circles, I've heard it stated that people can be "so heavenly minded that they are no earthly good."

One of my goals with this book is to flip that script. To help readers develop a mindset about heaven that is so compelling that it will lead readers into action and place people on a collision course with their next assignment from the Lord. I believe if we catch a glimpse of what heaven (and the beautiful build-up to heaven) looks like, it will cause us to put feet to our theology like never before. When we realize how beautiful, fulfilling, and eternal heaven is, we will be compelled to do our very best when on mission to see as many other people there with us as possible.

Depending on your age, you may have already experienced the realization that time is fleeting. When we are children or teenagers, old age and death seem as if they are an eternity away. However, the older we get, the more we realize that time is passing quickly, we have only one opportunity to live for the Lord in our fallen world, and before we know it, we will be standing before our Creator.

A systematic study of heaven will help us put all those things into perspective as we use Scripture and our God-given imaginations to view an accurate glimpse of heaven. To be reminded that the most important things are eternal things. Only what is done for Christ will last. And when we endeavor to understand our beautiful future in heaven, it reminds us of how close we are to our future and it should cause us to put that knowledge and understanding to practical use.

We're not there yet, but we're practically there, and I state that intending a twofold meaning. We're nearly there in the sense that through the lens of

Scripture, we can taste heaven with our imaginations. In another sense, the more we set our minds on things above (as this chapter's opening verse reminds us), the more we will realize that: spending our lives in pursuit of God's best is what matters most, earthly temptations are a destructive waste of time, unsaved people around us need to know Christ so they can join us in heaven, and the actions we take now in our temporal time will truly echo in eternity.

One who is truly heavenly minded will, in fact, be of tremendous earthly good!

Anything but Boring

I've noticed that many people envision heaven as a place where we'll peacefully sit around on clouds, playing harps for eternity. Honestly, that sounds more like hell to me. Humans long for adventure and exploration, for living out a story, for connecting with God and others on an ever-deepening level, and for enjoying true rest after a life well spent.

Now more than ever, Christians need a renewed biblical understanding of our amazing future. A proper understanding of where we will spend eternity and the remarkable events that will unfold leading up to it will help believers live with increased joy and anticipation as they serve God's purposes in this generation. It will also light a fire within believers, emboldening them to invite their friends and family members along with them to experience the mind-blowing future God has in store for those he calls his own.

If you think heaven might be boring, read the following verse slowly, carefully, and repeatedly. Let the truth of God's Word set in. In 1 Corinthians 2:9, we read, "'What no eye has seen, what no ear has heard, and what no human mind has conceived'—the things God has prepared for those who love him."

Ponder that verse for a moment. What is the most beautiful scene you have ever beheld? A 360-degree vista from the top of a mountain range? A sunset over the Grand Canyon? An underwater tropical reef teeming with life and vibrant with color?

What is the most beautiful sound you have ever heard? An orchestra playing a complex symphony? Birds chirping on a spring morning? An epic electric-guitar riff that stirs your soul and makes you feel alive? A newborn baby cooing contently? A houseful of children giggling and having fun?

Let's take it up a notch. What is the most beautiful thing you have ever imagined? Being able to fly without needing an airplane or parachute? Traveling to distant galaxies at the speed of thought? Reuniting with loved ones who have died and seeing them in their glorified eternal bodies? Being in the throne room of God, surrounded by billions of saved people and angelic beings singing praises to Almighty God? Hugging Jesus and beholding his nail-scarred hands with your very own eyes?

Nothing you or I have ever seen, heard, or imagined even comes close to how great heaven is going to be! May that heavenly mindedness cause each of us to truly live out our theology as we resist temptation, persevere when suffering, love the unlovable, and reach as many people as we can with the life (and eternity)-changing message that Jesus Christ died for them and secured a direct path for them to heaven!

The Theology of Heaven

As we embark on an in-depth, systematic, and practical study of heaven, it is important that we first reach bedrock. There are wildly conflicting views about heaven that are held to by various world religions, cults, and secular culture. We need a rock-solid baseline by which to compare all else. We need a standard. That standard is the Bible.

Important to any theological endeavor is an understanding of the foundational doctrine of bibliology—the doctrine of Scripture and revelation—or simply put, the doctrine of the Bible itself. In the study of bibliology, we learn that God reveals himself and his ways to his image bearers.

This leads to the five related doctrines of inspiration, inerrancy, authority, sufficiency, and canonicity. In short, this means that God has revealed truth to us through the inspired (literally "God-breathed") Word of God; it is without error, authoritative in its instruction, sufficient (providing everything we need to understand about God and our relationship to him), and complete (meaning the 66 books of the Bible contain God's full revelation).

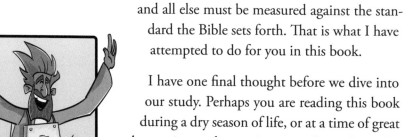

BIBLIOLOGY THE DOCTRINES OF SCRIPTURE

INSPIRATION: Deuteronomy 18:18-19; 1 Corinthians 2:12-13; 2 Timothy 3:16-17; 2 Peter 2:21; 3:1-2

INERRANCY: Psalm 119:142, 151, 160; John 17:17; 2 Peter 1:16, 19-21

AUTHORITY: Psalm 119:89; Isaiah 40:8; Matthew 24:35; 2 Timothy 3:16-17

SUFFICIENCY: Psalms 19:7-14; 119:105; Colossians 2:6-8; Hebrews 4:12; 2 Peter 1:3; Jude 3

CANONICITY: Ephesians 2:20; 1 Thessalonians 2:13; 2 Timothy 3:16-17; 2 Peter 1:3; 3:15-16; Jude 3; Revelation 22:18-19

All of that to say, our understanding and study of heaven must square with God's revealed truth as it is found in the pages of Scripture. Only what is revealed in the 66 books of the Bible should be used to form our theology, and all else must be measured against the standard the Bible sets forth. That is what I have attempted to do for you in this book.

I have one final thought before we dive into our study. Perhaps you are reading this book during a dry season of life, or at a time of great loss, pain, or disappointment. Or perhaps the slow and steady grind of life in a fallen world has you discouraged, as you look around and see what is taking place in our generation. These are yet additional reasons to learn more about our true home as believers. Studying the topic of heaven steels our nerves, recalibrates our mindset, encourages our spirit, and reminds us of why we are here. Our goal is to finish our race strong, and take as many people as possible with us to heaven!

The Non-Prophet

He's a Renaissance man. The ultimate throwback. The Non-Prophet is a 501(c)(3) that seems to have been born in 501 BC. He prefers the clothing, speech, food, grooming (or lack thereof), and customs of an archetypical Old Testament prophet living in twenty-first-century America. He misunderstands Bible prophecy and gives well-meaning but poor advice. The Non-Prophet is also not very wise with money, so he's a Non-Prophet on two levels. He's the epitome of the idiom "a day late and a dollar short."

SECTION 1:

HEAVENOLOGY—A SIMPLE SYSTEMATIC OVERVIEW

CHAPTER 1

Foundations

When they did not find them, they dragged Jason and some other believers before the city officials, shouting: "These men who have caused trouble all over the world have now come here, and Jason has welcomed them into his house. They are all defying Caesar's decrees, saying that there is another king, one called Jesus." When they heard this, the crowd and the city officials were thrown into turmoil.

ACTS 17:6-8

Millions of Christians around the world are persecuted in our day. In America, we have been graciously insulated from much persecution for the entirety of our nation's history. But for many believers in Africa, the Middle East, and various parts of Asia, persecution and martyrdom are the norm. If we look back through church history, we see how such persecution was present from the very start.

In the Bible, the book of Acts tells us about the very beginnings of the church. Part of that narrative shows us that for the early church, maltreatment was unrelenting. It includes details about the persecution of Christians, first at the hands of the religious leaders of Judea, and later at the hands of Caesar. One of the standout figures is Paul the apostle, who at first, was a persecutor of Christians (known then as Saul), but when he converted to Christianity, he took the gospel all throughout the Hellenized world, and all the way to Rome. By the conclusion of the book of Acts (and as attested to in Paul's letters), Paul was a prisoner of Rome, awaiting his own impending martyrdom.

But the persecution recorded for us in the book of Acts is only the tip of the iceberg. As the fledgling church grew during the first two centuries, it was primarily viewed as a minor distraction in a far-off region of the empire. However, once the Romans were faced with putting down two major Jewish rebellions, their sights turned toward Christianity as a potential cause of unrest and instability within the Roman Empire.

From AD 134 to AD 313, Christians suffered a horrific period of persecution and martyrdom filled with violence that remains unmatched in church history. Perhaps only in modern times, in places such as North Korea, Afghanistan, Somalia, Sudan, Libya, and others, have the levels of widespread torment been rivaled. But it all started in the first and second centuries, and a series of events mark the flashpoints when persecution was at its worst.

First, responding to the Great Revolt (AD 66–73), the armies of Vespasian campaigned in Judea seeking to restore stability in the area. His son Titus attacked and besieged the city of Jerusalem, ultimately leading to the city's downfall and the destruction of the temple in AD 70. The Jewish historian Josephus recorded that more than 1.1 million Jewish people were killed during that siege alone, a pivot point in the seven-year-long war. Then, in AD 132, a man given the name Simon bar-Kokhba claimed to be the Jewish messiah, and led a revolt that lasted from AD 132–135. It is known as the Bar-Kokhba rebellion. The Roman army also squelched this second uprising.

The Romans then decided to—once and for all—rid the empire of all things Jewish. An estimated 675,000 Jewish people from northern Galilee were killed, and many more were scattered to other lands. This would be the final (and might I add—prophesied) dispersion of the ancient Jewish people.

To ensure this was the last rebellion, Emperor Hadrian decreed that Jerusalem was to be renamed *Aelia Capitolina* and Judea would be renamed *Palestina*. The goal of the Romans was to wipe the Jewish people and their religion off the map. If that sounds familiar, it is because there is an end-times degree of antisemitism alive today that attempts to do the same.

In the early days of the church, Christianity was seen by the Romans as a sect of Judaism that was persecuted by the Jewish establishment. But after the Bar-Kokhba rebellion, Rome began to realize that although Judaism was decimated, the Christian offshoot (as they saw it) was not.

Worse yet for the empire, the Christians were turning many people into "atheists"—a term the Romans used to indicate that Christians didn't believe in the Roman gods and refused to worship them. The laws of Rome demanded that its citizens make sacrifices to Roman gods and worship the emperor as a god. A devout Christian could do neither.

The Roman Empire of Hadrian's day stretched from Scotland in the north to the Sahara Desert in the south, and from the Atlantic Ocean in the west to the

Caspian Sea in the east. From the Roman establishment's perspective, these lawless and disruptive Christians threatened the stability of the entire empire. Christians suffered increasingly horrific persecution, including such brutality as being killed in the Colosseum for sport, being fed to lions and dogs, being hung on crosses, and being used as torches. It was not until AD 313, when Emperor Constantine issued the Edict of Milan, establishing Christianity as an accepted religion of the Roman Empire, that levels of persecution began to wane under the Romans.

In most cases, the believer needed only to capitulate and state that Caesar was Lord, and then they would be spared. Yet thousands of Christians went willfully to their deaths rather than deny their Lord. Today, in many persecuted regions, Christians are given a chance to deny Christ and convert to avoid death. There are groups in Muslim countries that will demand conversion to the religion of Islam. Or in a country such as North Korea, where citizens are commanded to worship the Kim family as their god, loyalty to the state is what is exacted. Many faithful believers refuse and pay for it with their lives.

Our Devotion

What is it that drives such devotion and provides that level of resolve? I believe it can be attributed to two primary factors. First, a Christ follower's utter love and commitment for Jesus Christ. How could a believer reject or deny the One who laid his life down for them? A disciple's devotion to Christ springs from a thankfulness for what he has done, and our faith in his promises about what he will do in the future.

Second, I believe that Christians who lose their lives rather than deny their Lord realize more fully than most that this earth is not our final home. As believers, we are citizens of another place—mere ambassadors sent here to represent our true home as we invite others to join us there.

What is momentary suffering when we will have an eternity to spend with the Creator of all things? A proper biblical view of heaven that has made its way from our heads to our hearts will give us the strength to face anything that this world throws at us. We may never have to give our lives for our faith, but are we able to commit to living for our real home as we await our arrival there? Heaven is in our future—and it will be more than worth the wait.

People who hold to other belief systems show pious devotion to their religion or philosophy as well. Some are even willing to die for their beliefs. So, what separates Christianity from all other belief systems? This is an important question as we ponder the afterlife. Eternity is a long time. It is something we should want to get right.

The short answer is Christianity is the only teaching where the Creator dies on behalf of the creation. In every other religious system, the created beings—people—must perform in order to get right with the overarching deity. Or, in the case of some belief systems, humans are of no consequence at all. On a basic foundational level, Christianity provides the only grace-based foundations for faith. But let's dive deeper into more specific matters related to the subject of our study. What about other belief systems' various views on the afterlife? Does Christianity provide the best hope for the future in that regard as well?

According to a 2012 Pew Research Center study, in 2010, those who consider themselves Christians comprised 31.5 percent of the global population. Muslims sat at 23.2 percent. Unaffiliated people made up 16.3 percent. Hindus were 15 percent. Buddhists, 7.1 percent. Folk religionists (including African traditional religions, Chinese folk religions, Native American religions, and Australian aboriginal religions) collectively represented 5.9 percent. Other religions comprised about 0.8 percent. And Jews made up 0.2 percent.[2]

Additionally, in another Pew study conducted nine years later, the following results were found: 73 percent of US adults (of any faith or no faith) believe in heaven, and 26 percent do not believe in heaven or hell—though 7 percent of that last group do believe in "some kind of afterlife."[3] Real-world research confirms what Scripture says: "He has also set eternity in the human heart;

yet no one can fathom what God has done from beginning to end" (Ecclesiastes 3:11). These statistics show that what occurs after one's death is a topic of high importance to many, and it is something that every person should spend time considering.

Major Worldviews

So before we dive into a brief systematic overview of heaven, I want to address the 800-pound, postmodern gorilla in the room. In a historical and cultural moment when truth is seen as relative and every conceivable idea as valid, I think right now would be a good time to look at the biblical view of heaven in comparison to other worldviews that exist today. Specifically, what is the biblical backdrop for the doctrine of heaven in a truly Christian worldview, and what differences exist between that and the other viewpoints? Below is a brief description of the basic, historic core beliefs about the afterlife from the world's major religions:

Christianity

Here is a very basic overview of what the Bible tells us about the afterlife: It teaches there is an eternal afterlife in either heaven or hell; that no person is good enough to enter heaven on their own merit; that Christ's primary reason for coming to earth was to atone for sin and provide a pathway back to God; that heaven is a physical, literal, eternal, and supernatural place; and that hell is a place of eternal punishment and complete separation from God. Hell is depicted in such terms as outer darkness, fire, separation, and a place of weeping and gnashing of teeth (extreme regret). (You can read much more about what the Bible says about hell in chapter 12 of this book.)

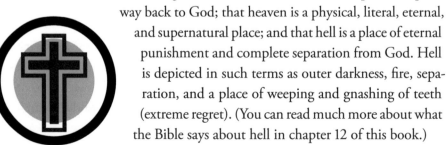

Judaism

Judaism relies primarily on the Torah (the first five books of the Old Testament) to provide insight about what is next for humankind, and it does not overtly reference the afterlife. Judaism does believe in the "next world," but the topic is rarely discussed in Reform, Conservative, or Orthodox Jewish circles. The Torah is seen in contrast to the ancient Egyptian's obsession with the afterlife, the context out of which the Torah was written by Moses. There is the general belief that because God is good, he will reward good people. The bottom-line teaching in Judaism is that followers must trust that the afterlife is in God's hands. So as a result, Judaism has vague and varying views about the afterlife.

Islam

Within every group or belief system there is a spectrum of belief, but here are the basic, widely held views about the afterlife that are commonly taught in Islam: It teaches there is an eternal heaven or hell; that good works must outweigh bad deeds in order for someone to eventually get to paradise; that paradise is characterized by endless spiritual and physical pleasure; and that hell is a literal and painful unending cycle of torture. Hell is the final destination for all non-Muslims.

Naturalism

Naturalism is the established philosophy and worldview of secularism and serves as the foundational framework for most governments, universities, secular education systems, and scientific organizations in academia. Naturalism teaches that humans are the result of completely random circumstances; humans have no ultimate meaning or purpose; people are merely bundles of chemical compounds that are animated by electrical impulses; and that humans simply cease to exist when their bodies stop functioning. It teaches that there is no heaven, no hell, no soul, no spirit, and no afterlife of any kind, and there is no ultimate accountability or judgment whatsoever.

Hinduism

Hinduism teaches that there are cycles of reincarnation that allow one to atone for sins from past lives until the soul is liberated (reaching Moksha) in order to merge with the god Brahma. When this occurs, there is no conscious eternal state for anyone. The end goal in Hinduism is to lose the sense of consciousness and become one with Brahma.

Buddhism

Similar to Hinduism, Buddhism teaches there are cycles of reincarnation that occur until humans can escape all cravings and desires. People do not have eternal souls, but their memories and feelings move forward to their next existence in the cycle of reincarnation. The goal is to reach nirvana, where a person's spirit merges with the divine.

BEST ON THE BLOCK

Best on the Block

So beginning with logic to build our case, here is how, in the cosmic neighborhood full of houses that hold to differing worldviews, the Christian view (based in Scripture) of the afterlife is the best on the block. Logically speaking, something *has* to be eternal. Logically speaking, something *had* to establish the laws of physics that govern the universe. Logically speaking, something *had* to be the First Cause that began everything. There simply is no way around those three fundamentally logical facts. Therefore, that *something* determined what the afterlife will be.

In addition to logic, philosophically and anthropologically speaking, humans throughout history have understood that something greater than us made everything, we are imperfect and inferior to God (however portrayed), we are eternal beings, and we need to somehow make up for our shortcomings to reconnect with God. Romans 1:20 describes this intuitive knowledge that all people possess. There, Paul wrote, "Since the creation of the world His invisible attributes, that is, His eternal power and divine nature, have been clearly perceived, being understood by what has been made, so that they are without excuse" (NASB). Every religion and belief system is an attempt to deal with these intuitive instincts.

Biblical Christianity is alone in the teaching that the Creator Himself suffered and died to save created beings. The core message of biblical Christianity is that God has made a single way back to himself that is offered to all humankind. Only Christianity offers salvation via a divine exchange whereby God himself paid the penalty for our sins so that we can be made right with him and live with him forever. It is the scandal of the cross whereby a sinner can be made righteous, where life-change begins with having one's debt paid in full, and where people can know their eternal destiny in advance because it is not based on their performance.

Christianity provides the only truly fair way to get to heaven. For every other world religion, a person's eternal destiny is dependent upon how they perform for God. Biblical Christianity is

the only belief system where a person's salvation is offered freely by a God who personally paid the price for it (John 3:16). It is not based on works but is received by grace (a free gift we don't deserve) through faith (believing on Christ) (Ephesians 2:3-9). The biblical Christian view of the afterlife is the best on the block because it is the only belief system that adequately answers all the logical, philosophical, and anthropological questions adequately.

And moving forward with that foundation, the Bible clearly teaches us that there is a heaven. In the next chapter, we are going to look at the background to heaven and why it exists in the first place.

CHAPTER 2

The Backstory of Heaven

Just as through one man sin entered into the world, and death through sin, and so death spread to all mankind, because all sinned.

ROMANS 5:12 (NASB)

Displayed in the Museo Nacional de Bellas Artes (National Museum of Fine Arts) in Buenos Aires, Argentina, is a painting by William Adolphe Bouguereau called *The First Mourning*. The title of the painting is a play on words. The beauty and uncorrupted nature of the first day when God created light itself is juxtaposed against the post-fall horrors of history's first murder.

The painting depicts a backdrop of grey, overcast skies and a barren landscape behind the figures in the foreground—Adam and Eve weeping over their slain son, Abel. Their grief is magnified by the fact that it was their own rebellion against God in the garden of Eden that introduced sin and corruption into the cosmos. It was their own disobedience that brought mortality to mankind, paving the way for one of their own sons to kill his brother.

Death Is Not Natural

The First Mourning speaks volumes to the downward spiral of sin and how thoroughly it has wrecked the universe. The painting succinctly captures the sentiment many have felt at a funeral or upon hearing the news of the unexpected death of someone they love. There is inherently something wrong about death. In our spirit, we sense that this is not supposed to be. It was not the original intention. Death is not natural.

Yet statistics consistently confirm that ten out of every ten people die. So this is an issue that carries importance for every person alive today. By the way, that means there is a very broad market for this book. The backstory of heaven is that death, decay, and separation were not part of the original plan. Thankfully, they are all done away with by the end of the story.

When I state that death is not part of God's original plan, I'm not positing that God was not aware of what was going to transpire after the six days of creation. He is omniscient and omnipresent. He knows all and is everywhere all at once. God is also sovereign. This means everything is under his control and there is not a single maverick molecule in the universe. So how can a sovereign God allow death to enter into the picture? And how can the free will humans possess change anything about God's original intended plan?

THE SOVEREIGNTY OF GOD

Theologians and philosophers have been wrestling with the tension between God's sovereignty and the free will of mankind for millennia. I address this tension in a couple of my other books, but to summarize: We will never fully reconcile the tension on this side of eternity because we are not God. We can't fit everything about who God is into the small space between our ears. We need to leave room for mystery and allow God to be God. In this life, we will never fully understand the answers to the questions above. We will need to exercise faith.

Unpacking the Backstory

I want to lay some groundwork and unpack the backstory of heaven before we consider the specific details the Bible shares with us about heaven in the coming chapters. As stated above, death, decay, and separation are not God's intention for humans' relationship with him. Even though we cannot comprehend it all, exploring the backstory of heaven will still help us to have increased clarity about the character of God and the existence of heaven.

When I state that I want to unpack the backstory of heaven, I'm alluding to the fact that the Bible is one grand narrative—one true historical (and yet-future) story. And here's the most amazing part: You are living in that story right now! From eternity past to eternity future, the narrative of Scripture lays out the historical scope of everything in between those two points. You and I are currently inhabiting the in-between. We look back to the cross to celebrate our redemption, and we look forward to the return of Christ as we await our glorious future in heaven.

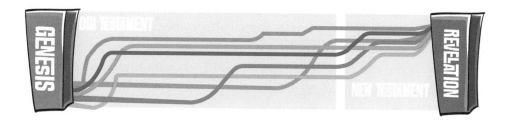

Eternity Past

God is revealed in Scripture as Father, Son, and Holy Spirit—yet as one. We refer to this as the doctrine of the trinity. Our triune God has existed this way from eternity past. The idea of a three-in-one monotheistic self-existent God is a great mystery to us—as is the nature of a timeless eternity past. Yet logic demands that something or someone has always existed. If anything exists, then something or someone has always had to exist. We know intuitively and logically that something cannot come from nothing. If anything is, something must be eternal. There is no way around that fact.

Creation

We can be certain that the self-existent triune God was not lonely or lacking in any way. He is eternally complete and unified in himself. God didn't lack anything. He was not in need. Yet something about his nature and perfection demanded that, at some point, the self-existent creator would create other moral autonomous beings—which he did. First, God created the angels, then he created humans.

Why did God do this? Well, I don't pretend to know all the ways of God, but here's one reason: Scripture informs us that "God is love" (1 John 4:8). It makes sense that God's nature should be manifested somehow. Here's what I mean: If God never created other beings, love could not have been expressed. If God created cookie-cutter robot beings programmed to obey, love could not be expressed. But if God created moral beings with the freedom to choose, God's nature could be demonstrated through their free-choice actions and ultimately through the sacrificial love he would personally demonstrate. Love, by definition, cannot be forced. Love must be freely given. This includes the possibility of love being withheld.

So although God lived in perfect peace and unity from eternity, his very nature required him to create everything *ex nihilo* ("out of nothing"), including moral beings with the ability to choose to follow God or to rebel against him. Though we may struggle now with the reality of evil and pain, one day, all will be made right and it will all make perfect sense.

This brings us to the creation account found in Genesis chapters 1–3. While this book addresses the subject of heaven, it is important to highlight the introductory aspects of all things, and those are laid out for us in the early chapters of Genesis. I believe in a literal six-day creation. God could have created everything instantly, but with God, there is always a purpose to the process.

It is clear in how God's special revelation (God's words to people) has been delivered to us that he wants us to know the foundations of the biblical narrative. While I can't address all of them here, one I want to focus on for the purposes of this book is that God's plan from the beginning was to dwell with the people he created in perfect unity and wholeness. The conditions present in the garden of Eden were literally perfect.

Eden is depicted in Scripture as a lush garden (Genesis 2:8; Ezekiel 28:13) and as a high mountain (Ezekiel 28:16). This mountaintop garden was (at one time) heaven on earth. It was a special place where a loving, relational God could live among his creation. We are told that God (likely the preincarnate Jesus) literally walked with Adam and Eve there (Genesis 3:8). Can you imagine having that kind of closeness and fellowship with the Creator of all things?

Eden was unlike anything we experience today. Adam and Eve dwelt in this original paradise where heaven and earth were one—and where God himself walked and talked with them. Isn't that what we all long for? Imagine perfect fellowship with God and each other happening in a perfect environment where evil, sin, darkness, decay, aging, pain, tears, fear, and separation do not even exist.

Fall

In Genesis 3, we read about the event whereby the close relationship between God and creation was severed. The serpent deceived Adam and Eve to break the one prohibition that was given them by the Lord. Once Adam and Eve took the bait, mankind fell into a state of brokenness and sin—the repercussions of which have sent shockwaves throughout all of creation and time. "The LORD God said, 'The man has now become like one of us, knowing good and evil. He must not be allowed to reach out his hand and take also from the tree of life and eat, and live forever'" (Genesis 3:22). For their own protection (and that of the future Savior), God had to drive Adam and Eve from the garden of Eden. God placed cherubim and a flaming sword to guard the only entrance back into Eden.

> Romans 5:12—Therefore, just as sin entered the world through one man, and death through sin, and in this way death came to all people, because all sinned.

For a time, the Creator would be separated from his image-bearers. The narrow, blocked entry into Eden would foreshadow a narrow, unblocked entry back to heaven for future generations who would come through Adam and Eve. There was only one way into Eden then, just as there is one way into heaven now. His name is Jesus.

> John 14:6—I am the way and the truth and the life. No one comes to the Father except through me.

The fall has impacted every aspect of life. So much so that we can't really grasp what a sinless universe would be like. Think about it for a moment. We live in a world where sickness and decay exist, where there is constant conflict and war, where we lock our houses and our cars, where caregivers and police are needed in every municipality, where hospitals and prisons are constructed and populated, and where the daily news highlights the impact that sin has on the world in real time. There is not a crevice of creation that sin has not degraded.

Redemption

Eden was where the fall occurred, but it was also the place where redemption began. God provided animal skins for Adam and Eve (Genesis 3:21), indicating that an innocent creature had to die and blood had to be shed to cover their sin. Though sin put separation between God and man—a redemptive theme began immediately and was progressively unveiled throughout

Scripture. It begins in Genesis and finds its ultimate fulfillment in the book of Revelation. Not only did God provide the animal skins that pointed toward redemption, he provided the first key prophecy about one who would secure that redemption!

> I will put enmity between you and the woman, and between your offspring and hers; he will crush your head, and you will strike his heel (Genesis 3:15).

I talk about this in my book *The Non-Prophet's Guide™ to Spiritual Warfare*. Where basically I said: In theological circles, the verse [Genesis 3:15]…is known as the *protoevangelium*. The Greek word *proto* means "original," and *evangelion* is the word for "good news." In Latin, it is translated *evangelium*. Genesis 3:15 is the original good news, or the first promise of a future redeemer—one who would defeat the lying serpent.

In this prophecy, the future redeemer is called the "offspring" (NIV) or the "seed" (NKJV) of the woman. This is the only verse in Scripture where a woman is said to have "seed," using the Hebrew word *zara* (zaw-rah). Applied elsewhere in Scripture, the root word *zera* is only used in reference to males or in an agricultural seed-planting context. This is an early indication that the Savior would be born of a virgin without any human male DNA.

Notice the offspring is a *he*, and according to the prophecy, *he* will be wounded—but ultimately, *he* will crush the head of Satan. From the moment this prophecy was given, the enemy's primary goal became eliminating the lineage of the future redeemer in order to keep God's prophecy from being fulfilled. If Satan was successful in his efforts, this would have saved his own head from being met-aphorically crushed, made God a liar, and brought Satan one step closer to stealing God's throne—or so he thought.

This single prophecy explains so much in Scripture and makes previously confusing events suddenly make crystal-clear sense. The motivation behind Satan's activity becomes very plain. In essence, Satan declared a seed-war. He has a constant obsession with destroying anything or anyone who might lead to the birth and ministry of the promised offspring of the woman, the redeemer.

Restoration

From a class I took in seminary, I recall a powerful exercise my professor assigned to all his students. We were embarking on a study of the Bible as one complete story of God designing a plan for his image-bearers to dwell with God and enjoy his presence in perfect fellowship forever. Our professor had us read Genesis chapters 1–2 and Revelation chapters 21–22, one right after the other. I encourage you to give this exercise a try.

REVELATION 21-22 = EDEN RESTORED

The common human practice is to mostly focus on the roller-coaster ride that came (and continues) as a result of the fall. Sin, decay, and brokenness permeate the universe and color every aspect of life. This has been true since the fall, and it will continue to be the case until the Lord returns to settle everything. We easily forget that we are in the middle of this great cosmic story. Our place in the timeline is in between the fall and the restoration of all things. The professor's exercise was a great reminder to cast our gaze forward.

In our discussion about heaven in this book, I thought it would be wise to point out that God's endgame is a fully restored universe where heaven and earth are one. That should be of great encouragement, even when you turn on the daily newscast and hear what seems to be nothing but an endless cycle of bad news.

So as you and I face the very real struggles of life on a personal level and as we witness the clear and present fallen nature of this world as it degenerates toward its prophesied end, we can have hope and we can take courage. What we see now is not what we will see in the future. In short, God has a game plan and he is right on track. Everything will be restored. When we but catch a glimpse of heaven in the present, it will sustain us until we experience it ourselves. Speaking of glimpses of heaven, now that we have the foundational backstory of a biblical view of heaven laid out, let's crack open the pages of Scripture and take a look at some glimpses of heaven that we know we have waiting for us!

CHAPTER 3

Glimpses of Heaven

In the year that King Uzziah died, I saw the Lord, high and exalted, seated on a throne; and the train of his robe filled the temple.

ISAIAH 6:1

In children's ministries circles, creative media is often used to assist teachers in relaying their lessons on topics and stories from the Bible. Video, music, animation, and other modern mediums are often used—at least in settings where those are possible. These and many other learning aids can help children grasp some of the basic truths from God's Word.

But before all of these, many children's Sunday school teachers utilized a learning tool known as the flannelgraph. You may recall one of your own teachers using one of these, or perhaps you've seen pictures of them. They are a thin piece of fairly lightweight wood covered in a light-colored flannel material. This large flannel board is placed on an easel or a wall so the whole group can see it. Artwork that sticks to the flannel on the board is used to tell the story. As the teacher reads the account or tells the story, they place or remove the artwork of backdrops, characters, and props on and off the flannelgraph to help drive the story home visually. By necessity, the stories are simplified to their most basic and easily understandable form for the young audience and per the medium used.

For example, the flannelgraph story of Jonah might include artwork of the main character

Jonah, a few secondary characters, a whale, a small boat, a storm cloud, the city of Nineveh, and other relevant props. The narrative can be presented and followed, and God's patient and forgiving character can be highlighted in application. However, illustrative learning aids are not perfect and can only take you so far.

While such aids can help with visualizing some aspects of the book of Jonah, they fall short of conveying concepts beyond what can be seen with the eyes. Jonah's prayer from chapter 2 and his anger toward the Lord in chapter 4 are a little more difficult to capture using visual media, so unfortunately, they can get abandoned from the lesson altogether. If children never study the account of Jonah on a deeper level as they grow and mature in their faith, they are left with holes, inaccuracies, poor theology, and no personal application or connection to the rest of Scripture.

Flannelgraph Theology

As believers, it is easy for us to adopt a disjointed and anemic flannelgraph theology when it comes to the afterlife or other complex themes in Scripture. In one of my seminary courses, we discussed the fact that there are levels of theologians. While this sounds a bit heady and pompous at first glance, when you think about it logically, it makes total sense—and is completely necessary.

First, everyone is a theologian. If you have ever thought about our origins, God, the afterlife, or the related concepts of right and wrong—you are a theologian. Next, there are necessarily at least four types or tiers of theologians: folk theologians, lay theologians, professional theologians, and academic theologians.

Folk theologians develop their convictions by pulling bits and pieces from what they have heard or learned. This is sort of a bird's-nest theology made up of concepts and ideas from various sources but not very systematic or holistic in its approach—and understandably so. Pre-Christians and new believers are usually folk theologians.

Lay theologians are usually believers who have walked with the Lord for a while, experienced some years of life, studied the Bible fairly in depth on their own, and volunteered in a church or ministry organization leading others in Bible study of one sort or another. Lay theologians often teach folk theologians. It is part of the process of discipleship.

Professional theologians are pastors and other paid ministry staff who have had some focused Bible training, and likely have been to Bible college or seminary. They have studied the Bible more holistically and systematically than the lay theologian. Professional theologians often help disciple and train lay theologians.

Finally, there are academic theologians. Their purpose is to train and equip professional theologians. Therefore, they often have quite a bit more specialized training in a specific area of theology—and often significant real-world, hands-on ministry experience of their own.

Why bring all of this up? Well, when it comes to heaven (and many other complex or often misunderstood areas of theology), many of us believers have more of a folk theology or a flannelgraph theology. Because we're so busy dealing with our daily lives and since we know as believers that our future in heaven is secure, we may be tempted to just leave it at that.

Or we pull pieces together from what we've learned and heard, like building our bird's nest, but we still have lingering questions about heaven, hell, and even the nature and process of salvation that remain unresolved. So the purpose of this chapter is to share the key passages about heaven to demonstrate what heaven is like now, and what heaven will be like in the future.

It may surprise you to learn that heaven, in its current state, is an intermediate version that exists in the unseen realm. It may also surprise you to learn that believers who have died are in an intermediate conscious state in the presence of the Lord. The current heaven and the intermediate state of believers await the culmination of all things, when God will create the new heavens and the new earth, and the new Jerusalem will come down out of the unseen realm (Revelation 21:1-3). Here, God will literally be present with humankind again, similar (but better) to what we read about the garden of Eden.

INTERMEDIATE

So this chapter, along with the previous chapters, serve to set up a basecamp for us from where we can climb to higher altitudes to explore what key coming events and the final state of heaven will be like in our not-too-distant future!

Where Did Old Testament Believers Go?

The Old Testament speaks of the righteous dead going down to *Sheol* (usually translated as "the grave"). But you may be thinking, *Aren't the righteous supposed to go to heaven when they die?* This has caused confusion for many and has also led to some faulty theology, most notably the concepts of soul sleep and purgatory. Soul sleep teaches the idea that when believers die, their souls sleep until after judgment day, when they will wake up in heaven. Purgatory teaches that while Jesus' sacrifice paid for some of our sins—our basic sin nature, so to speak—we must still spend some time in hell to pay for our other sins before being ushered into heaven later. Both of these concepts are errors that go against the specific and clear teaching of Scripture.

I Peter 3:18—For Christ also suffered once for sins, the righteous for the unrighteous, to bring you to God. He was put to death in the body but made alive in the Spirit.

> 2 Corinthians 5:6-8—Therefore we are always confident and know that as long as we are at home in the body we are away from the Lord. For we live by faith, not by sight. We are confident, I say, and would prefer to be away from the body and at home with the Lord.

As seen in the verses above, when we read the New Testament, we are given more information that helps clear up the confusion. In the Old Testament, God's people looked forward to the promise of a Savior because Jesus had not yet come. Though they were made right with God through faith in the promise of a future Savior, legally speaking, their sins were not yet paid for. The prophesied transaction was as good as done but it had not actually occurred yet in history.

So the righteous dead remained in a heavenly holding place until such time that the promise was actually fulfilled. Whenever the righteous died during the time period prior to the cross, they went to a section of *Sheol* (Hebrew)/ *Hades* (Greek) known as paradise or Abraham's side. The word *side* used here is the Greek word *kólpos*.

There really is no English equivalent to *kólpos* so it is difficult to translate. This was an overhanging fold of the outer garments worn at the time that formed a small pocket area near the chest. The *kólpos* is essentially a special area that is synonymous with intimacy, union, comfort, and protection. It carries connotations of a baby being swaddled or a toddler sitting on their father's lap. This special position of comfort and blessing is the general meaning of Abraham's side.

Prior to the cross, all of the righteous dead went to this comforting and blessed holding place of promise. We read about it in Luke 16. In this chapter, Jesus shares an account that sheds tremendous light on the subject. It is important to note that this was not a parable but is described as an actual account.

In verses 19-26, we read,

> There was a rich man who was dressed in purple and fine linen and lived in luxury every day. At his gate was laid a beggar named

Lazarus, covered with sores and longing to eat what fell from the rich man's table. Even the dogs came and licked his sores.

The time came when the beggar died and the angels carried him to Abraham's side. The rich man also died and was buried. In Hades, where he was in torment, he looked up and saw Abraham far away, with Lazarus by his side. So he called to him, "Father Abraham, have pity on me and send Lazarus to dip the tip of his finger in water and cool my tongue, because I am in agony in this fire."

But Abraham replied, "Son, remember that in your lifetime you received your good things, while Lazarus received bad things, but now he is comforted here and you are in agony. And besides all this, between us and you a great chasm has been set in place, so that those who want to go from here to you cannot, nor can anyone cross over from there to us."

So we learn a few new things from this passage. Angels escorted Lazarus to paradise (Abraham's side). The rich man, who was not right with God, ended up in a lower section of Sheol/Hades. This is what we would refer to today as hell. It is characterized by torment, agony, fire, loneliness, and an awareness of the blessing of the righteous dead. We also learn that people's positions are fixed and there is a great chasm or gulf between the place of blessing and the place of torment.

Where Are Old Testament Believers Now?

During his earthly ministry, Jesus told us where he was going to go during the time between his death and resurrection. In Matthew 12:38-42, we read,

> Some of the Pharisees and teachers of the law said to him, "Teacher, we want to see a sign from you." He answered, "A wicked and adulterous generation asks for a sign! But none will be given it except the sign of the prophet Jonah. For as Jonah was three days and three nights in the belly of a huge fish, so the Son of Man will be three days and three nights in the heart of the earth."

While interpreters' positions vary widely and this is admittedly a very difficult passage to handle, it appears that perhaps Jesus went to Sheol/Hades (mentioned above). In 1 Peter 3 (also a difficult passage with various interpretations), we're given some potential insight about what Jesus did during those three days. In verses 18-20, we read,

> Christ also suffered once for sins, the righteous for the unrighteous, to bring you to God. He was put to death in the body but made alive in the Spirit. After being made alive, he went and made proclamation to the imprisoned spirits—to those who were disobedient long ago when God waited patiently in the days of Noah while the ark was being built. In it only a few people, eight in all, were saved through water.

And Ephesians 4:8-9 sheds further light on Jesus' interaction specifically with the righteous dead in paradise/Abraham's side. There, Paul tells us,

> This is why it says: "When he ascended on high, he took many captives and gave gifts to his people." (What does "he ascended" mean except that he also descended to the lower, earthly regions? He who descended is the very one who ascended higher than all the heavens, in order to fill the whole universe.)

So it appears likely that during the three days between Jesus' death and resurrection, this was the time frame in which he went down to Sheol/Hades, declared there that mankind's sin was now paid for, took the righteous dead from paradise into heaven where God dwells, and gave them gifts. We can only speculate, but perhaps the gifts given to these Old Testament believers may have been similar to the eternal rewards church-age believers will be given in the future at the bema seat of Christ (see chapter 5). I cite Deu-

teronomy 29:29 again here to remind us that there are details in Scripture that will have to wait for a full explanation until we are in heaven. But it makes sense to me that God would similarly reward these Old Testament believers.

Luke 23 details the final hours of Jesus' life. You may recall, when Jesus hung on the cross, one of the criminals being executed beside him believed in him, and Jesus told the man, "Truly I tell you, today you will be with me in *paradise*" (Luke 23:43). In other words, Jesus was highlighting the fact that both he and the believing criminal were about to die, but afterward, they would both be comforted at Abraham's side, the place of paradise.

God's promise had been kept. The prophecies of the Messiah and his atoning death had been fulfilled. This was a game changer on many levels, not the least of which was the location of the residence of righteous believers who had died prior to the time of the cross. The cross set the wheels in motion. Because of that single event, paradise changed zip codes and moved to heaven, where God dwells.

But what about church-age believers? What about the resurrection of the righteous, spoken of in Daniel and in the New Testament? We will answer these questions in coming chapters, but first, let us continue our journey through the various details related to the intermediate state of heaven.

Does Satan Have Access to Heaven?

I address this in detail in my book *The Non-Prophet's Guide™ to Spiritual Warfare*, but it is worth discussing this question briefly here in case you have not read that book or studied this topic. We discover some details about Satan's access to heaven in the book of Job. In Job 1:6 and 2:1, we learn that after the fall, Satan has had a type of restricted access to the realm of heaven, only when summoned by God.

Apparently, there are legal formalities, a hierarchical structure among angels (whether fallen or holy), and certain points of time when God has summoned Satan to the heavenly realm to serve God's purposes. What you are about to read is purposely redundant for effect. God is *so sovereign* that even Satan will ultimately be used for God's glory and our good.

Satan's multipart fall from heaven (detailed in the book mentioned above) will ultimately result in his being thrown into the lake of fire, where he will suffer eternally. Until then, things are ordered in an intermediate state. The earth is temporarily title-deeded to the enemy, whom Scripture calls "the prince of this world" (John 14:30) and "the god of this age" (2 Corinthians 4:4). Note the lowercase *g*! Satan is not God's equal. He is a created being subject to the will and plans of the Creator. When God restores all things, this will include the complete and exact punishment of all evil.

Glimpses of the Throne Room

The few depictions Scripture gives us of the throne room of God have more to do with God's presence than his location. As you'll see from the snapshots below, God's throne moves with him. Something we can take away from this is we can be confident he is always in control. No matter how chaotic things get here, God is sovereign over the affairs of history and the details of our lives.

Ezekiel 1:4-28

Ezekiel, in his vision, saw what seems to be a mobile throne room of sorts, supported and transported by cherubim—a higher class of divine beings with characteristics of angels, humans, and animals, representing all of God's created order. This was a vision of God on the move. The floor of the throne room is seen as a transparent, sparkling crystal plane that supports God's mighty throne (which is apparently a vibrant blue color, like a lapis lazuli gemstone) on which the intense light of our holy God blazed forth, encircled by a heavenly spectrum of colors. The many details convey God's majesty, omniscience, omnipotence, utter holiness, and sovereignty. This passage is a lengthy one, but I have included it in the text here because the majesty of it all should not be missed:

EZEKIEL

> I looked, and I saw a windstorm coming out of the north—an immense cloud with flashing lightning and surrounded by brilliant light. The center of the fire looked like glowing metal, and in the fire was what looked like four living creatures. In appearance their form was human, but each of them had four faces and four wings. Their legs were straight; their feet were like those of a calf and gleamed like burnished bronze. Under their wings on their four sides they had human hands. All four of them had faces and wings, and the wings of one touched the wings of another. Each one went straight ahead; they did not turn as they moved.
>
> Their faces looked like this: Each of the four had the face of a human

being, and on the right side each had the face of a lion, and on the left the face of an ox; each also had the face of an eagle. Such were their faces. They each had two wings spreading out upward, each wing touching that of the creature on either side; and each had two other wings covering its body. Each one went straight ahead. Wherever the spirit would go, they would go, without turning as they went. The appearance of the living creatures was like burning coals of fire or like torches. Fire moved back and forth among the creatures; it was bright, and lightning flashed out of it. The creatures sped back and forth like flashes of lightning.

As I looked at the living creatures, I saw a wheel on the ground beside each creature with its four faces. This was the appearance and structure of the wheels: They sparkled like topaz, and all four looked alike. Each appeared to be made like a wheel intersecting a wheel. As they moved, they would go in any one of the four directions the creatures faced; the wheels did not change direction as the creatures went. Their rims were high and awesome, and all four rims were full of eyes all around.

When the living creatures moved, the wheels beside them moved; and when the living creatures rose from the ground, the wheels also rose. Wherever the spirit would go, they would go, and the wheels would rise along with them, because the spirit of the living creatures was in the wheels. When the creatures moved, they also moved; when the creatures stood still, they also stood still; and when the creatures rose from the ground, the wheels rose along with them, because the spirit of the living creatures was in the wheels.

Spread out above the heads of the living creatures was what looked something like a vault, sparkling like crystal, and awesome. Under the vault their wings were stretched out one toward the other, and each had two wings covering its body. When the creatures moved, I heard the sound of their wings, like the roar of rushing waters, like the voice of the Almighty, like the tumult of an army. When they stood still, they lowered their wings.

Then there came a voice from above the vault over their heads as they stood with lowered wings. Above the vault over their heads was what looked like a throne of lapis lazuli, and high above on the throne was a figure like that of a man. I saw that from what appeared to be his waist up he looked like glowing metal, as if full of fire, and that from there down he looked like fire; and brilliant light surrounded him. Like the appearance of a rainbow in the clouds on a rainy day, so was the radiance around him (Ezekiel 1:4-28).

Isaiah 6:1-4

In Isaiah's commissioning vision, we are given another glimpse of God—this time, with seraphim hovering over the Lord. The job of these angelic beings seems to be to shine a spotlight on God's holiness. The praise of these divine beings was so powerful that it shook the entire heavenly throne room. Read the brief passage below:

ISAIAH

In the year that King Uzziah died, I saw the Lord, high and exalted, seated on a throne; and the train of his robe filled the temple. Above him were seraphim, each with six wings: With two wings they covered their faces, with two they covered their feet, and with two they were flying. And they were calling to one another: "Holy, holy, holy is the LORD Almighty; the whole earth is full of his glory." At the sound of their voices the doorposts and thresholds shook and the temple was filled with smoke (Isaiah 6:1-4).

Revelation 4:1-11

Finally, I would like to direct you to the biblical account that contains the most complete depiction of the throne room. It is found in Revelation 4. Scholars debate whether verse 1 is a depiction of the rapture of the church, or simply John's invitation into the vision where he would be shown the details of the future events of the tribulation period. Applying either interpretation, it's clear that John is first taken to the throne room in heaven to remind him that God is sovereign over history, even during the chaos of the Day of the Lord, which is also known as the seven-year tribulation period or Daniel's seventieth week (see Daniel 9:27).

In this passage, we're not told the color of the throne, but God displays his redemptive nature by showing up as sparkling red—now that the ultimate sacrifice has been made and Jesus is glorified. The 360-degree rainbow is again depicted, as are a few other details that we read about in Ezekiel and Isaiah. Take a few moments to read the full passage here:

> After this I looked, and there before me was a door standing open in heaven. And the voice I had first heard speaking to me like a trumpet said, "Come up here, and I will show you what must take place after this." At once I was in the Spirit, and there before me was a throne in heaven with someone sitting on it. And the one who sat there had the appearance of jasper and ruby. A rainbow that shone like an emerald encircled the throne. Surrounding the throne were twenty-four other thrones, and seated on them were twenty-four elders. They were dressed in white and had crowns of gold on their heads. From the throne came flashes of lightning,

rumblings and peals of thunder. In front of the throne, seven lamps were blazing. These are the seven spirits of God. Also in front of the throne there was what looked like a sea of glass, clear as crystal.

SERAPHIM 1

SERAPHIM 2

SERAPHIM 3

SERAPHIM 4

In the center, around the throne, were four living creatures, and they were covered with eyes, in front and in back. The first living creature was like a lion, the second was like an ox, the third had a face like a man, the fourth was like a flying eagle. Each of the four living creatures had six wings and was covered with eyes all around, even under its wings. Day and night they never stop saying: "'Holy, holy, holy is the Lord God Almighty,' who was, and is, and is to come."

Whenever the living creatures give glory, honor and thanks to him who sits on the throne and who lives for ever and ever, the twenty-four elders fall down before him who sits on the throne and worship him who lives for ever and ever. They lay their crowns before the throne and say: "You are worthy, our Lord and God, to receive glory and honor and power, for you created all things, and by your will they were created and have their being" (Revelation 4:1-11).

After Jesus' ascension we find him placed at the right hand of the throne of God (Hebrews 8:1; 12:2; Revelation 3:21). And in Revelation 4, we see an additional 24 elders (whom I believe to be key church leaders or representatives of the church) present in the divine council/throne room.

While these visions of the throne room provide merely a small glimpse of heaven as it currently exists, they do reveal some key attributes about the nature of God's dwelling place in the unseen. While we currently reside in the timeframe in between mankind's fall and final restoration, the snapshots above provide a few vivid previews of heaven's command center—almost as though we have been momentarily admitted through the back door of God's headquarters and into the center of his sovereign activity. Indeed, the central feature of heaven (even in the future eternal state) is the very presence of God. As I mentioned in the previous chapter, God's final plans include a fully restored universe where heaven and earth are one, and where God will literally dwell with humans.

Full Circle—Eden Restored

Recall that, originally, heaven and earth were melded in a major way. Eden is pictured in Scripture as a mountaintop garden where God interacted directly with mankind (Genesis 3:8). The fall of man fractured that original setup. In modern-day mathematic and comic book lingo, the dimensions were now fractured, resulting in a parallel dimension that exists alongside of ours. The final two chapters of the book of Revelation concern the restoration of the world to an Edenic state, putting things back to the way God originally intended. (We'll look at this in greater detail in chapter 9.)

In between right now and the future new heavens and new earth, where God will once again dwell in our midst, there will be several important events that occur for believers in Christ. These include the rapture, the judgment seat of Christ, the wedding supper of the Lamb, the return of Christ to earth, and the millennial kingdom.

These are all key milestones leading up to the final eternal state, yet few people venture to study them in depth. If you have placed your faith in Christ, these are all literal events that you will personally experience. As we prepare for this amazing journey, let's familiarize ourselves with the landmarks along the way to our eternal destination. In the next section, we will delve into all of them. So put your seat belt on, place your gaze out the window, and get ready for one amazing trip!

SECTION 2:

TIMELINE TOWARD ETERNITY

CHAPTER 4

Mismatched Socks and 17-Year Cicadas

After that, we who are still alive and are left will be caught up together with them in the clouds to meet the Lord in the air. And so we will be with the Lord forever.

1 THESSALONIANS 4:17

How's that for a strange chapter title? I'll share two quick stories, and then it will all make sense. First, a comical but true story from my wedding day. When it comes to the event of a wedding, everyone knows that the center of attention and the person everyone really wants to see is the bride—complete with the custom-tailored elegant wedding dress, meticulously done hair and makeup, the carefully arranged floral bouquet, and an entourage of brides-maids and others tending to her every need.

This is why there are feelings of great anticipation experienced by the family, the invited guests, and most importantly, the groom, waiting for the first moment that they will see the bride. When the leading few notes of *Canon in D* start playing, the crowd instinctively stands and looks to the back of the church to catch their first glimpse of the bride who has been preparing for hours—I mean years—for this momentous event.

By the same token, the groom also gives a lot of attention to special preparation for the big day. However, the groom's dedication and formal ensemble will never garner equal fervor and anticipation to that of the bride. Grooms usually wear rentals, tuxedos recently worn by other grooms, prom-goers, and the like. The groom is not waiting in the wings before he is seen. Rental-boy is at the front of the altar, awaiting the bride's appearance just like everyone else.

Well, when I rented my tux, I was glad it came with everything I needed, or so I had thought. It had a jacket, shirt, bow tie, cummerbund, cuff links, fancy buttons, and pants with easy-to-use sizing clamps so the monkey suit could be readjusted for the groom who had the same tux rented for the following week's wedding. But one thing the rental didn't come with was socks. And that makes sense. It would be kind of gross to wear socks that some random guy wore the week before.

Due to this much-appreciated hygienic practice, I grabbed a pair of socks that I had stuck in the depths of my sock drawer way back who knows when. And when I got to church and started to get ready, I realized I had brought a pair of mismatched socks. One, black and thin. The other, dark blue and thick. Oh, brother. But matching socks or not, to cite the well-known theater motto, "The show must go on."

So there I was, alone in the basement of United Baptist Church putting on some mismatched socks by myself while my soon-to-be wife was upstairs with her entourage getting ready with close attention paid to every small detail. But being the groom, my focus was not on myself. I had invited my fiancée to spend her life with me. I wanted this moment to be special for her.

We had both waited for this moment for a full year. All the planning, all the coordinating, all the invitations to family and friends, all the anticipation, and now the moment was finally here! As the music began to play and the synchronized sound of a few hundred people standing up from the creaky wooden pews momentarily filled the room, I knew. I knew life would never be the same. I knew another season was about to begin. I knew a new life awaited us as two were united as one.

Nearly 24 years (at the time of writing this chapter), three "kids" (now adults), and a daughter-in-law later, getting married remains the best decision I've ever made—second only to my decision to follow Christ.

This admittedly makes for a strange transition, but let us momentarily flashback about 12 years before the mismatched socks. I grew up in the Washington, DC area and distinctly remember the first time I witnessed the 17-year Brood X cicadas emerge and take over the entire metro area for a few weeks. In 1987, I was 16 years old, so these large clumsy flying bugs had not yet appeared in my lifetime. The last time that they had surfaced was the year before I was born. I had heard stories about the cicadas, but I was 16 when I first witnessed them with my own eyes. And when they surfaced, these giant mutant winged bugs were everywhere—hitting windshields, flying into cars and causing accidents, and being crunched underfoot as people walked on the sidewalks and streets. It was like nothing I had ever seen.

When I was much younger, I would occasionally find the shell of one of these bugs still clamped onto tree branches or trunks. When I would inquire about them, my father would tell me about the 17-year cicadas. What I saw as a kid were merely the several-year-old discarded skins of the 1970 cicadas that outgrew their exoskeletons during the rapid growth they experienced in their short lives.

Whenever the 17-year cicadas surface, the females lay eggs inside slits in small branches of trees. These eggs hatch into nymphs six weeks later and fall to the ground. Next, they burrow into the darkness of the ground and feed on root systems for 17 years. Finally comes their metamorphosis when they emerge from the ground and crawl up trees to attach themselves to a branch, where their skins split and fully developed cicadas emerge. After taking a few moments to get used to the brightness of their new world, they fly off to start the whole process all over again.

Tying Tuxes and Transformation Together

Now, let me tie these two seemingly disconnected stories together. Jesus is our bridegroom. The church—every true believer in Christ since the day of Pentecost—is the bride. The New Testament uses a Jewish wedding motif throughout to highlight the amazing, mysterious, and supernatural union between Christ and the church.

In John 14:1-3, Jesus said,

> Do not let your hearts be troubled. You believe in God; believe also in me. My Father's house has many rooms; if that were not so, would I have told you that I am going there to prepare a place for you? And if I go and prepare a place for you, I will come back and take you to be with me that you also may be where I am.

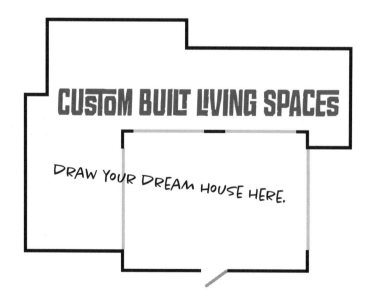

CUSTOM BUILT LIVING SPACES

DRAW YOUR DREAM HOUSE HERE.

This passage captures the essence of the Jewish wedding tradition of Jesus' day. In first-century Judea, a son would pick a bride, then his father would pay a great price for her, sort of an ancient dowry. The marriage proposal would be offered to the potential bride, and she would either accept or reject it. If she accepted, the son would go back home to his father's house and either build an addition onto the house or build a separate small house on the same property.

Later, when the living space was ready and the son's father thought the time was right, he would tell his son to go and get his bride. The bride would not know the day or the hour of the son's coming, but she would always stay ready because she knew her groom could come at any time.

The groom would usually be preceded and announced by his groomsmen and, upon the groom's arrival, the bride would literally be swept off her feet and carried on a platform back to the father's house, where the wedding would commence. After the official ceremonies, the bride and groom would enter the wedding chamber for seven days while the wedding party continued outside during that time. At the end of the seven days, the bride and groom would emerge to begin their new live together.

With that bit of cultural history in mind, reread the passage in John 14 above and note the clear and unambiguous wedding motif Jesus used. Often when Christ spoke of his return, this wedding motif would be employed. Similarly, when the writers of the various letters of the New Testament wrote about the return of Christ, this same focus was present.

Jesus chose a bride, the church. The Father paid a great price; he gave his only Son (John 3:16). During the church age (the age in which we are now), individuals can either accept or reject Christ. Jesus went back to the Father's house, where he is building our custom-built living spaces. And at the Father's

foreordained time, he will send the Son to go and get his bride and bring her to the Father's house—the rapture of the church.

In the Father's house (heaven), the bride will remain for seven years (while the tribulation period is taking place on earth). There, she will be permanently united with Christ and receive wedding garments. At the end of the seven years, the Groom will lead the bride back to earth to begin their new life together in the millennial kingdom. The order of eschatological (end times) events and the ancient Jewish wedding tradition line up perfectly!

Consider this: If Jesus created the universe in six days, can you imagine what our specially prepared living spaces are going to look like if he has been building them for nearly 2,000 years?! My fellow believer, the next amazing surprise and prophetic event the Lord has in store for you is the rapture! Titus 2:13 calls it our "blessed hope." First Thessalonians 4:18 says we are to encourage one another with the doctrine of the rapture as we long for the Groom to come and claim his bride. We often forget that the Groom longs to be with the bride as well!

Right about now you may be wondering about the cicada story above. *What in the world do cicadas have to do with weddings?* you ask. Do the demonic locusts of Revelation 9 descend on the wedding and wreak havoc? No need to fret; my reason for telling you my cicada story is much more positive and encouraging.

In 1 Corinthians 15:51-52, Paul states, "Listen, I tell you a mystery: We will not all sleep, but we will all be changed—in a flash, in the twinkling of an eye, at the last trumpet. For the trumpet will sound, the dead will be raised imperishable, and we will be changed."

The subject Paul addresses in 1 Corinthians 15 is the resurrection. At the resurrection, we will have new and glorified spiritual bodies, like the one Christ has. First John 3:2, says, "When Christ appears, we shall be like him." For church-age believers, this will occur at the moment of the rapture. Paul details this in slow motion for us. In 1 Thessalonians 4, Paul provides a frame-by-frame description of the events of the rapture.

In 1 Thessalonians 4:15-17, we read,

> According to the Lord's word, we tell you that we who are still alive, who are left until the coming of the Lord, will certainly not precede those who have fallen asleep. For the Lord himself will come down from heaven, with a loud command, with the voice of the archangel and with the trumpet call of God, and the dead in Christ will rise first. After that, we who are still alive and are left will be caught up together with them in the clouds to meet the Lord in the air. And so we will be with the Lord forever.

God clearly makes known to us that we will receive new bodies and tells when this will occur for believers of the church age. Now combine the two illustrations. We see the rich details of the ancient Jewish wedding motif coupled with the fact that we will receive new glorified bodies fit for heaven. Just as the root-eating wingless cicadas had to dwell underground in darkness until their metamorphosis, we dwell in fallen bodies awaiting the rapture, when we will be changed and able to handle the glories of heaven—including flying, traveling at the speed of thought, entering rooms without opening doors, and much more!

So what about believers who have died during the church age? Where are they

now? The answer is they are with Christ in spirit form. Back up a verse in 1 Thessalonians 4, and it clearly states that "God will bring with Jesus those who have fallen asleep in him" (verse 14). Those who are with Christ now await the rapture, when they will receive their glorified spiritual bodies as well. They are currently in an intermediate heaven (more on that later), existing in an intermediate state. But they are fully conscious, enjoying God's presence (Philippians 1:23-24), and they are completely sinless (Romans 7:24-25).

The Bottom Line

Who?

Who is going in the rapture? Scripture is clear that "we will all be changed" (1 Corinthians 15:51). *All* means *all*. There is no caste system in Christianity. It is all or nothing. One soldier may not have the same level of maturity or dedication of another soldier, but they are both in the same army.

Anyone who has truly accepted Christ will go in the rapture. The nature of sin is that none of us realize how deeply wrecked by it we really are, even when we recognize that its consequence is death. The nature of grace is that Jesus paid it all. There is absolutely nothing we can do to earn salvation. Also, there is nothing we can do to lose it. Now, we can still suffer relational breakdown and discipline if, after repentance, we wander from the Lord. But if someone is saved—even if only for a millisecond before the rapture occurs—they will be

"ALL" OF THE BELIEVING WILL BE LEAVING!

caught up in the rapture. It is true that there are degrees of blessing based on what we do for the Lord (more on that in the next chapter), but every single church-age believer will be resurrected or raptured when that trumpet is blown.

What?

The rapture is when the universal church will instantaneously be taken up to heaven. This will include all believers who are alive on the earth at that time and the resurrection of all church-age believers from the grave. The term *rapture* refers to a catching away, a sudden taking up of all true believers to be with the Lord. The English word *rapture* comes from *rapturo*, which

is from the Latin translation of the New Testament Greek word *harpazo*. *Harpazo* is found in the key biblical text concerning the rapture, 1 Thessalonians 4:13-18. First Corinthians 15:51-52 is another passage that sheds light on this mysterious event.

When?

Scripture repeats the fact that only God knows the "day or hour" of the return of Christ (Matthew 24:36), and in turn, the rapture. The rapture is a signless, imminent event. It could happen at any time. There are several verses that support the doctrine of imminence. For example: Philippians 3:20; 1 Thessalonians 5:6; 2 Timothy 4:8; Titus 2:11-13; James 5:8; 1 John 2:28; and 3:2. Yet every year there are those who predict a day on which the rapture will occur. So far, there has been a 100 percent failure rate.

The bottom line is, no one knows the day or hour, so we all must remain ready. This readiness can be illustrated by looking at the lives of athletes from the sport of boxing. Boxers are not always aware of when their next opportunity to land a paid boxing match will be, so most successful boxers have a motto, and it is this: "If you stay ready, you won't have to get ready." Following a match, rather than allowing themselves to get out of shape, then having to train for months to get back into shape (or lose an opportunity to win), most fighters live a lifestyle of readiness.

Boxers train regularly whether they have a fight lined up or not. They don't want to get caught unprepared. That is how the believer should live every day. Jesus told us to keep ready: "Keep watch, because you do not know on what day your Lord will come" (Matthew 24:42). That being said, Scripture does tell us that we can "see the Day [of the Lord] approaching" (Hebrews 10:25), but we'll discuss that later in this book.

Where?

All over the world. Can you imagine what that moment will be like? When graves will burst open wherever believers have died, then millions of Christians are suddenly taken to meet the Lord in the clouds? You live in a generation that witnessed the near-immediate global impact of COVID-19. Can you imagine the aftermath of the rapture? This single event will be the first domino that sets all other end-times events into motion.

Why?

The rapture will occur to fulfill prophecy, set all end-times events into motion, bring the church (the bride) to Jesus (the Groom), and allow God to return his primary attention back to his program with the Jewish people. Just as the church had a mysterious and sudden beginning on the day of Pentecost, it will have a mysterious and sudden end at the moment of the rapture.

God has one mega-story of redemption, but within that overarching narrative there are several eras, epochs, or dispensations. The church age is one of them. In the upcoming chapters, we'll discuss the final era of redemption known as the kingdom age, which will be followed by the eternal state (the final state of heaven).

How?

The resurrection and rapture church-age believers will experience will not be figurative or spiritual. It will be literal and physical. The God who created the universe knows where every molecule is located, and he created everything out of nothing. The resurrection of the dead and the rapture of the church will be no problem for our God, who is all-powerful.

What About the Various Views?

I know this is a book about heaven, but as we chronicle the events leading up to the eternal state of heaven and cover the doctrine of the rapture, you may be wondering why I hold to the pretribulation view of the rapture. Taking this position, I believe the rapture will happen prior to the future seven-year tribulation period, and that the church will not have to go through that period on the earth.

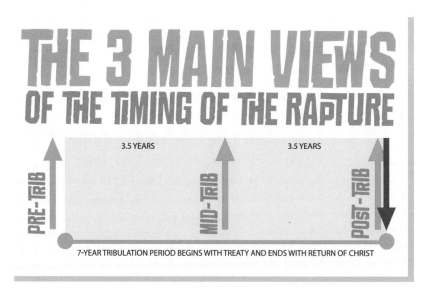

THE 3 MAIN VIEWS
OF THE TIMING OF THE RAPTURE

PRE-TRIB

3.5 YEARS

MID-TRIB

3.5 YEARS

POST-TRIB

7-YEAR TRIBULATION PERIOD BEGINS WITH TREATY AND ENDS WITH RETURN OF CHRIST

I cover this at length in other books, but I want to share seven basic reasons why I believe the pretribulation rapture is clearly taught in Scripture. It is not a salvation issue, nor is it an issue we should divide over, but it is an important issue nonetheless. So here are seven (of the many) reasons why I believe in a pretrib rapture.

1. We Are Not Appointed to Wrath (1 Thessalonians 5:9)

This and many other verses clearly say we are not appointed to wrath or that we will escape the coming wrath. In fact, Revelation 3:10 clearly states that the church will be kept *from* (Greek word *ek*, meaning "out of," not "through") the hour of trial *that will come upon the whole earth*. The entire tribulation period is God's wrath. Jesus opens the seals, and by the sixth seal judgment, the inhabitants of earth clearly state they know they are experiencing God's wrath (Revelation 6:15-17).

2. The Tribulation Period Is Daniel's Seventieth Week

Context is key, and the original framework for the tribulation period (and all things end times) comes from Daniel 9, which lays out all of Jewish history, including the fact that the final seven years of world history will refocus on the Jewish people. In other words, the main purpose of the future tribulation period is not focused on the church. In further support, the church is mentioned some 18 times in the first three chapters of Revelation, but not once after the judgments begin in chapter 6.

3. Jewish Wedding Traditions

We already discussed this earlier in the chapter, but I want to recap this and point out that all of the symbolism related to end-times events mirrors ancient Jewish wedding traditions. Jesus used that tradition as an illustration in his teachings. In ancient Jewish wedding traditions, the groom would leave his father's house, travel to the desired bride's home, pay a great price for the bride, have his offer accepted or rejected, become legally bound if accepted, and go back to his father's house to prepare a place for his bride.

At a specific time known only to the father, the son would be sent to go get his bride. The groomsmen would announce the groom's arrival, then the bride would be lifted up onto a special seat to be carried away with the groom. The couple would enter the wedding chamber for seven days, and then there would be a great wedding feast after the marriage was consummated.

Space does not allow here, but every single one of those details lines up with the order of key first-coming and second-coming events. Again, here is one key passage, this time from the New King James Version: "In My Father's house are many mansions [i.e., custom-built living spaces]; if it were not so, I would have told you. I go to prepare a place for you. And if I go and prepare a place for you, I will come again and receive you to Myself; that where I am, there you may be also" (John 14:2-3 NKJV, insert added).

4. Imminency

The clearly taught doctrine in Scripture is that the Lord could return at any time without any preconditions. This can only be true of the pretrib view.

5. Our Blessed Hope

Titus 2:13 calls the rapture our "blessed hope." It is what we're looking forward to. Nowhere does Scripture tell Christians to prepare to endure hell on earth. Every mention of the Lord's return is painted as something we look forward to with joyous anticipation. During the tribulation, most believers—people who will have placed their faith in Christ after the rapture—will be martyred. That is not a "blessed hope."

6. Old Testament Types

Two judgments we see in the Old Testament clearly prefigure the final time of God's wrath on earth: the flood of Noah's day, and the judgment of Sodom and Gomorrah. In both cases, God removed those he promised to save prior to judgment being carried out. There are many other types and figures in Scripture that point to this pattern as well.

7. The Rapture Is Designed to Encourage

In the main text on the rapture, 1 Thessalonians 4:13-18, Paul concludes by saying, "Therefore encourage one another with these words" (verse 18). That statement simply makes no sense apart from a pretrib rapture.

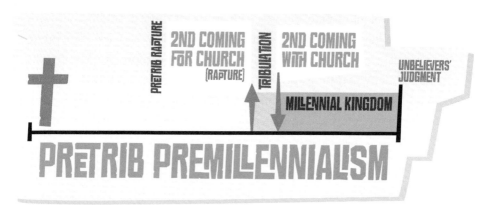

You Must Be Crazy!

The rapture of the church will be the most significant global event since the flood of Noah's day. None of us has ever witnessed a rapture. So how do we know it is really going to happen? Believe it or not, the once well-established doctrine of the rapture is under attack in our day from within the church. Talk about friendly fire!

As you can see from the verses above, the Bible clearly teaches that there will be a rapture. Believers can debate the timing of this future event, but I want to say, as bluntly as I can, that those who teach that there will be no rapture are denying a truth that is clearly stated in the Bible.

Scripture is unambiguous about this guaranteed future event. But how do we know it will happen as foretold? Because God's track record is perfect. Did you know that nearly 80 percent of the prophecies in the Bible have already been fulfilled? They were fulfilled with 100 percent accuracy, down to the detail. The remaining 20 percent (or so) of yet-future prophecies—such as the rapture—will in like manner be fulfilled.

God gives us a built-in proof of authenticity. Trusting God for the fulfillment of the rapture is not a blind leap of faith, but a faith based on reason, facts, and God's perfect track record of fulfillment. He is a promise keeper. He is sovereign. He is all-powerful. He is all-knowing. We can fully trust that this event is on the near horizon.

What an exciting thing to await, the culmination of our salvation and the consummation of our marriage. I can almost hear the heavenly version of *Canon in D* begin to play. It sounds a lot like a trumpet, a shout, and a command. Stay ready so you won't have to get ready. The Bridegroom is coming soon!

But what will we do when we get there? If you haven't studied this before, it will blow your mind. Take a deep breath, then turn the page and find out.

CHAPTER 5

Heavenly Rewards

We must all appear before the judgment seat of Christ, so that each of us may receive what is due us for the things done while in the body, whether good or bad.

2 CORINTHIANS 5:10

If you have seen the movie *Schindler's List*, you may recall a scene near the end when World War II has ended, and Oskar Schindler (played by Liam Neeson), who had rescued at least 1,100 Jewish people, is about to say good-bye to them. They present him with a ring as a token of their appreciation.

At that moment, a thought hits him. He could have done more. He could have saved more people. Lamenting, he considers: Why did he keep his car? It could have saved ten more people. He pulls a pin off his jacket that could have saved one more person. The thought of *one more person* then consumes him as he breaks down and weeps in regret.

In that moment, though Oskar Schindler had done so much good, he realized that there were no do-overs, no going back in time, no more opportunities to save another person from the horror of the Nazi concentration camps. In the film, as he weeps, many of the Jewish survivors he saved encircle him and embrace him, trying to assuage his grief.

This scene serves as a powerful picture of the judgment seat of Christ, also known as the bema seat. It is a judgment for believers where we will give an account for what we did in light of our salvation. To be clear, salvation is a free gift God offers to mankind, accomplished through the sacrifice of his Son to anyone who would believe (1 John 2:2). There is absolutely nothing we can do to earn salvation on our own or lose it once we are saved.

But once saved, we remain responsible for our motives, thoughts, and actions—particularly how we used the gifts, abilities, and opportunities that we have been given.

As Jeff Kinley states in his book *Wake the Bride,*

Your salvation was sealed in Him and He declared you eternally righteous before Him. As a result, there is not an ounce of wrath or a drop of anger waiting for you in heaven. Not one sin will be brought up at the bema. To do so, Jesus would have to deny the efficacy of His own death and resurrection, not to mention contradicting His word and character. Salvation is complete. You are guilt-free. Jesus paid it all.[4]

So rest assured that the judgment seat of Christ is not a place where God will show a movie of your life to the rest of the church-age believers. It's not a tool for shaming or embarrassing us. While our ticket to heaven has already been paid for by Jesus on the cross, there is still great incentive for us to dedicate our lives to his work while we await his return or our own death. The judgment seat of Christ, in Greek, is known as the *béma* seat. In the ancient world, the *béma* was a raised platform where judges sat to award athletes with special wreaths (i.e., crowns) after a competition. As we will see in a moment, while there may be a momentary sense of regret at opportunities we missed, the primary purpose of this future heavenly event is to be rewarded for our service to Christ while in the body on earth.

We learn more about the details of this event in 1 Corinthians 3:11-15, where Paul wrote,

> No one can lay any foundation other than the one already laid, which is Jesus Christ. If anyone builds on this foundation using gold, silver, costly stones, wood, hay or straw, their work will be shown for what it is, because the Day will bring it to light. It will be revealed with fire, and the fire will test the quality of each person's work. If what has been built survives, the builder will receive a reward. If it is burned up, the builder will suffer loss but yet will be saved—even though only as one escaping through the flames.

Among the rewards given are what Scripture refers to as *crowns*. Whether these crowns are literal crowns or represent certain levels of responsibility and oversight (or both) I'm not sure, but there are at least five crown rewards mentioned in the Bible. Likely, we will also be given various opportunities to rule and reign with Christ in the millennial kingdom (Revelation 20:4-6) based on what work we accomplished while here on earth (see Matthew 25:14-30).

INCORRUPTIBLE CROWN
1 Corinthians 9:25-27

CROWN OF LIFE
Revelation 2:10

CROWN OF GLORY
1 Peter 5:2-4

CROWN OF RIGHTEOUSNESS
2 Timothy 4:8

CROWN OF REJOICING
1 Thessalonians 2:19-20

Second Corinthians 4:14 gives us a hint at the chronology of the events. There we read, "We know that the one who raised the Lord Jesus from the dead will also raise us with Jesus and present us with you to himself." As we established in the previous chapter, the rapture is the resurrection for church-age believers, and this verse notes that after the resurrection we are presented to God. It makes sense that the first order of business after the beautiful heavenly events of the rapture is to stand before Christ to receive our rewards.

This is something we should look forward to and something that helps us persevere through the trials we face in life. Notice a couple of verses later (and still in the same context) we read this in verses 17-18: "Our light and momentary troubles are achieving for us an eternal glory that far outweighs them all. So we fix our eyes not on what is seen, but on what is unseen, since what is seen is temporary, but what is unseen is eternal."

Another proof text that supports the chronology of the bema seat rewards following the rapture is found in Revelation 22:12, where Jesus declares, "Look, I am coming soon! My reward is with me, and I will give to each person according to what they have done."

Support for the idea that the bema seat rewards may include levels of responsibility in the future millennial kingdom is found in Matthew 25:14-30, where we read Jesus' parable of the bags of gold. If you have time, pause, and read it for context.

To summarize, a man went away on a journey and left his wealth with his servants to invest for him. Upon his return, he rewarded them with greater responsibility based on how they invested what was entrusted to them. One important note is that the last servant (who did not do anything with what was given to him) represents the unbeliever. Notice in verse 30 that he was to be thrown "outside, into the darkness, where there will be weeping and gnashing of teeth." In other verses in the New Testament, this is language that is used to describe hell (more on this in chapter 12).

So this final servant did nothing with the gift of salvation. Therefore, he had no part in the kingdom. While we will face momentary regret by opportunities lost as believers, that is nothing compared to what people will experience when they do nothing with the momentous sacrificial gift that has been offered them through Christ's work on the cross.

Also, there is further application to this parable and its relationship to salvation and our future rewards. Notice that all of the servants who accepted the gift also put the gift to work. In the sixteenth century, the great reformer

MARTIN LUTHER

Martin Luther thought that the book of James was included in the canon of Scripture by mistake because it highlights the importance of works—James 2:14-26 in particular. Verse 26 says plainly, "Faith without deeds is dead." In Martin Luther's view, this contradicted what the letters to the Romans and the Ephesians taught about salvation by grace alone, through faith alone.

But the point James was trying to get across was not that we are saved by faith *plus* works, but rather, that we are saved by a faith *that* works. The natural outflow of our salvation is that our lives will be characterized by a desire to work hard at the things that are important to Christ. The subjects of the kingdom want to work for the purposes of the King!

QUICK FACT: DID YOU KNOW...
that all of Jesus' parables point to the future Millennial Kingdom?

That is in view here with the parable of the bags of gold. The natural outflow of accepting the gift of salvation is that we will put the gift to work. Neglecting to act on the gift is proof that one is not of the kingdom. Humans can't see a person's heart or motives, but God can. He knows who are truly his and those who are not. All of this will one day be revealed.

There's one more thing I want to be sure to note before we move on. Do not think for a moment that the rewards of heaven await only pastors, missionaries, and well-known evangelists. Some of the greatest rewards may well be saved for those who worked tirelessly, sacrificially, quietly, and humbly behind the scenes.

The rewards a believer will receive will be associated with motive and overall mission. The person who prays for a pastor, gives to missions, or stuffs envelopes for a faithful ministry will get to take part in their reward. Matthew 10:41 states, "Whoever welcomes a prophet as a prophet will receive a prophet's reward, and whoever welcomes a righteous person as a righteous person will receive a righteous person's reward."

Each believer will be rewarded based on how they leveraged the spiritual gifts, opportunities, and abilities they received—not based on the perceived impact of what they did. Jesus' lesson in Luke 21:1-4 captures this concept. There, we read, "As Jesus looked up, he saw the rich putting their gifts into the temple treasury. He also saw a poor widow put in two very small copper coins. 'Truly I tell you,' he said, 'this poor widow has put in more than all the others. All these people gave their gifts out of their wealth; but she out of her poverty put in all she had to live on.'"

Living in Light of Heavenly Rewards

In the 2006 film *Invincible*, which is based on a true story, the life of Philadelphian Vince Papale (played by Mark Wahlberg) depicts the tale of an inspiring underdog. In the 1970s, Papale had fallen on hard times both relationally and financially. He hadn't had much go his way, and South Philadelphia was hit with tough economic times. Even their beloved Eagles had not had a decent season in quite some time. Despite all of this, Papale was a die-hard Philadelphia Eagles fan and season ticket holder.

The newly hired coach of the Eagles, Dick Vermeil (played by Greg Kinnear), made the unprecedented decision to hold open tryouts that allowed anyone to come and compete for a spot on the team. Initially, this was more of a publicity stunt to get the fans excited than it was an actual tryout. But Vermeil was surprised by 30-year-old Papale's speed and talent. At the end of the day, only one person was given an opportunity to continue trying out for the team—Vince Papale.

Papale played with tremendous heart, making it through several cuts and eventually making the roster for the season. To do so, he had to persevere through weeks of rigorous training, endure being disliked by other veteran members of the team, and overcome the discouraging aspects of his past and his financial situation.

That season, the Eagles lost all their preseason games and their opener against the Dallas Cowboys. Papale's life in the National Football League did not look promising—until game two of that season, when the Eagles played the New York Giants at home. In that game, Papale had a tremendous special teams tackle on the opening kickoff. And later, he had another impressive tackle that caused a fumble by the Giants, allowing the Eagles to clinch the win.

Papale went on to play with the Eagles for three seasons and even became a team captain. He was the oldest non-kicker rookie in the history of the NFL and still holds that record to this day. While the movie took some creative license to make Papale's story fit the screenplay model and make for an entertaining movie that would attract audiences and earn money at the box office, the fact that Papale played with courage, grit, and determination was absolutely real. To earn his spot, he had to *leave it all on the field*. This phrase means that a contestant plays without reservation, without holding back—like a soldier who fights until they have nothing left.

A player who leaves it all on the field is one who understands the importance of the moment and does not want to let the occasion pass them by with any regrets. They understand that this opportunity will not come around again. They grasp an understanding that their chance to make a difference is a one-time offer.

What if we carefully weighed every choice, every spoken word, every action as if we were going to give account for it one day? Because we will. Again, this judgment will not be for salvation but for giving an account for what we did with our salvation. We have the best news ever to share and the best perspective to leverage our gifts for God's purposes.

In light of heaven, in light of our knowledge of the future judgment seat of Christ, in light of all that Jesus did on the cross to bear our sins, it is time for us to leave it all on the field! Heaven and eternal heavenly rewards await us. And what is mind-boggling is that the bema seat is just the first stop on our tour of heavenly events. It's only the beginning!

CHAPTER 6

A Truly Heavenly Wedding

Hallelujah! For our Lord God Almighty reigns. Let us rejoice and be glad and give him glory! For the wedding of the Lamb has come, and his bride has made herself ready. Fine linen, bright and clean, was given her to wear.

REVELATION 19:6-8

The older I get, the more I sound like my dad. He used to say things that were witty and a little corny. But now all these years later, I find myself gravitating toward the same humor and I must admit, I love dad jokes. Once my kids (who are grown now) were old enough to know what a dad joke was, every joke I've told thereafter has been categorized as a dad joke. In my defense, I could tell the greatest joke on the planet, and it would still be labeled a dad joke. Further proof of this phenomenon is that my kids can tell the very same joke, but for some reason it is not categorized as a dad joke. Be that as it may, I have a few good wedding and marriage dad jokes that would be really fitting for this chapter, but I'll spare you (and my "kids") the torture.

However, I will pass along a dad joke that was shared by the officiant who married my wife and me, Pastor Koch. At our rehearsal dinner, opening his short speech, he said, "Do you know what the purpose of a wedding ring is?" (Insert long pause here.) "It's to cut off your circulation." Then he went on to share how Tracey and I had decided to "cut off our circulation" and become one, as husband and wife. He went on to share that biblical marriage is designed to be permanent, and how it serves as a picture of Christ and the church.

This intended permanence is why so much time, planning, and finance is put into most weddings. Great sums of money are spent on flowers, food, flights, tux rentals, bridesmaids' dresses, and the pinnacle of the expenditures—the bride's wedding dress. The all-important wedding dress is so significant that extravagant figures are spent on this single-time-worn outfit.

One article cites that the most expensive wedding dress to date was one worn by tennis star Serena Williams in 2017. It cost $3.5 million. The next closest (according to the article) was Queen Elizabeth II's dress in 1947, which was purchased for $42,000 (equivalent to $1.6 million today).[5]

In many cultures that have been historically influenced by Christian thought, particularly the West, the wedding dress has always been white. Have you ever wondered where this comes from or why that is the case? It is taken directly from Scripture. The verses at the opening of this chapter set the cultural precedent for white wedding gowns, Revelation 19:6-8. In Scripture, particularly in the book of Revelation, the white wedding garments are associated with the finalization of the marriage between Christ and the church in heaven.

A basic outline for the book of Revelation is as follows: the first chapter sets the framework for the entire book, chapters 2–3 contain seven letters from Christ to the church, we catch a glimpse of God's throne room in Revelation chapters 4 and 5, then chapters 6–19 show the calamities of the tribulation period, and as mentioned previously, Revelation ends with the millennial kingdom (chapter 20) and the new heaven and new earth (chapters 21–22). We discussed this briefly in chapter 3, but here I want to zero in on the heavenly wedding details that are present in a couple of places in Revelation. These give us insight into what we will experience after the judgment seat of Christ.

The Wedding Ceremony

Immediately following Revelation 4:1, when John was taken up to heaven, we see him present in the very throne room of God. My personal belief is that Revelation 4:1 is a depiction of the rapture. There is an open door in heaven, a voice, and a trumpet. These details line up with 1 Corinthians 15:52 and 1 Thessalonians 4:16 (the two key rapture passages), and the chronology fits as well.

Furthermore, once in the throne room, John sees 24 elders with gold crowns who are dressed in white. Many commentators agree that the 24 elders represent the church. They are either 24 key church figures, or simply 24 representatives of all believers from the entire church age.

We also find that John sees the seven lampstands, now in heaven. This is significant because we're told in Revelation 1:20 that the lampstands represent the churches. The churches and lampstands are seen on earth in Revelation 2 and 3, but after Revelation 4:1 they are depicted in heaven.

In Revelation 4:5, we read, "In front of the throne, seven lamps were blazing. These are the seven spirits of God." This also lines up with 2 Thessalonians 2:6-7, where we're informed that the future antichrist cannot be revealed until after the restrainer is removed (i.e., the Holy Spirit-indwelled church is raptured).

It makes sense that we will receive our crowns (and whatever other eternal rewards the Lord may have planned for us) immediately upon entering heaven following the resurrection/rapture. We're not given specific details on how this will take place, but given the fact that there will potentially be billions of Christians who appear before the judgment seat of Christ (2 Corinthians 5:10) and that the wedding itself (between Christ and the church) will also have to take place within a few short earth years (the seven-year tribulation), somehow all of this will need to transpire rather quickly.

Perhaps God's omnipresence and the timeless nature of heaven play a factor in how this is accomplished. It is possible that each believer simultaneously will have their own personal moment with the Lord at the judgment seat of Christ. It is also likely that one of the rewards we will receive at the judgment is our heavenly clothes, or what John refers to as our wedding garments. It makes logical sense to have a personal moment with Christ and receive our rewards just prior to the wedding ceremony, or perhaps as part of it. In any case, those details are not revealed, and we must leave room for mystery and let God be God. The bottom line is that we cannot explain everything in Scripture and must accept many things by faith.

What Scripture does reveal is that both the judgment seat of Christ and the official marriage of Christ to his church will take place in heaven while the seven-year tribulation period is taking place on earth. Supporting this is the fact that when Christ returns at the end of the tribulation period, Revelation 19:8 depicts the church returning with Christ with their wedding garments on. Then Revelation 19:14 depicts "the armies of heaven" (angels and the church) returning with Christ "dressed in fine linen, white and clean."

One commentator notes the likelihood of proximity between the moment of the rapture and the official wedding. Regarding Revelation 19:7, Dr. Thomas Constable notes, "The bride is the Lamb's newly married wife having been joined to Him in heaven immediately after the Rapture. This is, by the way, the third of three metaphors in Revelation that describe women: the woman (mother) in chapter 12 is Israel, the prostitute in chapter 17 is Babylon, and the bride in chapter 19 is the church."[6]

> Revelation 19:7—Let us rejoice and be glad and give him glory! For the wedding of the Lamb has come, and his bride has made herself ready.

Now, I must admit something here. As a man, I can't fully relate to the wedding metaphor employed by the Lord to give us a picture of the beautiful relationship between Christ and the church. To get to the point—I do not feel very manly picturing myself as a bride. But as I'll unpack later in this book, the clear and beautiful application of the metaphor is that Christ and the church can't wait to be together.

Think for a moment about the fact that God chose you from before the foundation of the world (Ephesians 1:4), left the glories of heaven to become a human (though he never ceased to be God) (John 17:5), was willing to die for you even though you were a rebel (Romans 5:8), suffered and died to redeem you from the curse (Galatians 3:13), was separated from the Father (try to figure that one out) on your behalf (Matthew 27:46; Mark 15:34), and after his resurrection, went back to heaven, where he has been preparing a custom-built heavenly living space for you (John 14:2-3).

If you are a believer, I want you to take some time to think about one of the most touching moments you have had with the Lord. Think of a moment when you felt overwhelmed with your love for him. I've had several of those moments in my life—usually in times of prayer or while reading (or talking about) a particular verse. They are moments where I felt I could almost touch heaven. Moments when I felt I would be willing to do anything for the Lord, who so graciously gave his very life for me on a bloody, rugged, cruel Roman cross.

Now consider the moment when you will get to see the Lord face to face. When you will see the holes in his hands and feet. When you will lay your crown at his feet in an act of sheer worship and know that you are safe, protected, forgiven, and truly loved—forever. That, my brothers and sisters, is what the metaphor of the bride and the Bridegroom represents. Jesus longs to be with us just as much as we long to be with him.

The Wedding Supper

There is one more feature to this amazing future wedding that the church will experience in heaven, but it appears that this part won't actually take place in heaven at all. It is known as the marriage supper of the Lamb.

Opinion is split as to where the marriage supper will take place. Some Bible expositors hold to the view that this part of the wedding event will take place in heaven, some others believe it will take place on earth, and still others think that it will begin in heaven and then continue on earth after the return of Christ to the earth. I tend to agree with Dr. Ed Hindson (now with the Lord) and Dr. Ron Rhodes, who say this will indeed take place on earth after the antichrist's armies have been vanquished.

Hindson states, "Some suggest a difference between a marriage supper in heaven and a later marriage feast on earth. Others, myself included, view the marriage as taking place in heaven and the marriage supper taking place when Christ returns, extending into the millennial kingdom when both Jews and Gentiles will be invited and celebrate with the Lord."[7]

Rhodes gets even more specific and places the marriage supper within a 75-day period (see Daniel 12:11-12). He says, "The marriage supper of the Lamb takes place on earth sometime later [i.e., after the marriage ceremony], apparently during the 75-day interval between the end of the tribulation period and the beginning of the millennial kingdom."[8]

Logically speaking, it makes great sense for the order of events following the rapture to be the judgment seat of Christ, followed by the marriage ceremony, followed by the wedding supper during the 75 days before the kingdom age.

JEWISH WEDDING TRADITIONS
AND CHRIST AND THE CHURCH

BETROTHAL	LEAVE FATHER'S HOUSE	JESUS LEFT HEAVEN
	TRAVEL TO DESIRED BRIDE'S HOME	CAME TO EARTH AS A BABY
	PAY A GREAT PRICE FOR THE BRIDE	DIED ON THE CROSS FOR OUR SINS
	OFFER ACCEPTED OR REJECTED	OFFERS SALVATION TO US
	MARRIAGE CONTRACT/LEGALLY BOUND TOGETHER	IF WE ACCEPT WE BECOME THE CHURCH ("BRIDE OF CHRIST")
	GROOM BACK TO FATHER'S HOUSE TO PREPARE HOME	JESUS HAS GONE BACK TO PREPARE A PLACE FOR US
WEDDING	FATHER SENDS SON BACK WHEN ALL IS READY	GOD KNOWS THE "DAY AND HOUR" HE WILL SEND THE SON
	GROOMSMEN ANNOUNCE GROOM'S ARRIVAL	THE ARCHANGEL WILL SHOUT AND A TRUMPET WILL BLOW
	BRIDE IMMEDIATELY TAKEN BACK WITH GROOM	THE CHURCH/BRIDE OF CHRIST WILL BE RAPTURED
	THE TWO ENTER WEDDING CHAMBER FOR 7 DAYS	THE CHURCH WILL BE IN HEAVEN DURING THE TRIBULATION
	GREAT WEDDING FEAST AT END OF 7 DAYS	THE CHURCH WILL ATTEND THE WEDDING FEAST OF THE LAMB

(Right side labels: 1ST COMING OF CHRIST / RAPTURE AND CHURCH IN HEAVEN DURING TRIBULATION PERIOD)

We are betrothed to Christ and await his return to whisk us away in the rapture. Upon arrival at the Father's house we will receive reward and be officially married. Then we will celebrate with others who are invited to the wedding supper. Together, we will rule and reign with Christ in the kingdom.

One additional detail that needs a bit of unpacking is the question of who the other people are who are invited to the wedding supper of the Lamb. Revelation 19:9 reads, "Then the angel said to me, 'Write this: Blessed are those who are invited to the wedding supper of the Lamb!'"

These wedding feast guests are Old Testament saints and tribulation-era saints. The rapture is for the church only, but the other faithful will be resurrected at the end of the tribulation (also likely to take place during the 75-day interval).

Additionally, those Jewish people (see Zechariah 13:8-9) and new believers who will have survived the tribulation will enter the millennial kingdom in their natural bodies to repopulate the earth during the kingdom age (more on this in chapter 8).

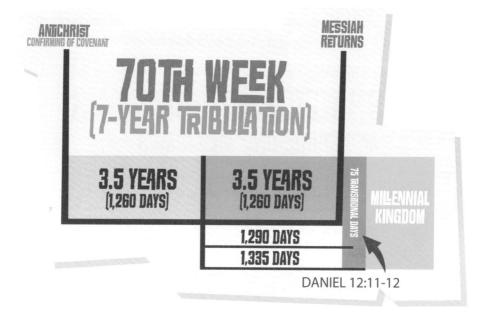

ANTICHRIST CONFIRMING OF COVENANT

MESSIAH RETURNS

70TH WEEK (7-YEAR TRIBULATION)

3.5 YEARS (1,260 DAYS)

3.5 YEARS (1,260 DAYS)

75 TRANSITIONAL DAYS

MILLENNIAL KINGDOM

1,290 DAYS

1,335 DAYS

DANIEL 12:11-12

Literally the Perfect Wedding

Even the best weddings on earth have things that go wrong. At our wedding, one small miscommunication caused a large (but ultimately manageable) mishap. We invited everyone we knew to the wedding, but only specific people were invited to the reception. As planned, at the end of the wedding ceremony, instructions were given to follow the bride and groom to the reception venue. However, these instructions lacked a critical clarifying phrase at the beginning. The missing opening phrase was, "If you have an invitation to the reception…"

The omission of these eight words led to the arrival of an additional 50 people to our reception. This was an issue because space, seating, and food were required to accommodate the unplanned attendance of another four dozen or so of our closest friends.

No matter how much planning and preparation takes place in the months leading up to the big day, there are always unlikely outliers, unexpected challenges, unforeseen details, or factors that are out of our control that present themselves. Some of these mishaps or surprises are more significant than others, but inevitably there is always something that pops up.

The same is true for earthly marriages. Though Christian couples should do their best to honor their vows and reflect the union between Christ and the church in their relationship, we live in a fallen world that is marred by sin. Marriages that go the distance must weather the ebb and flow of life, the challenges that face being a family in a fallen world, and the spiritual growth that comes with being committed to one person for a lifetime.

A dear friend of mine, the late Dr. Ed Hindson, spoke at a conference I attended just a few months before he went to be with the Lord. He was a professor and dean at Liberty University for many years, and in a message he gave at the conference, he shared how oftentimes students would come to him asking if they should feel guilty for not wanting the rapture to occur yet. They were young and wanted to get married and have children. There was so much they wanted to experience and hadn't yet.

Dr. Hindson wisely pointed out to them that once Christians arrive in heaven, there will not be a single believer who wishes that they could go back and experience anything they may have missed. Heaven is perfection—the culmination of everything our hearts long for in this world.

Dr. Hindson also added (somewhat comically) that many of these students who longed to be married and have families would often return about five years later asking if he thought the rapture would be coming any time soon.

All of that to say, even the best earthly marriages have their challenges, imperfections, and trials. But the future mysterious union of Christ and the church will be a perfect union. This heavenly union will be unmarred by sin and the corruption and decay that are the effects of sin. It will be the epitome of perfect fellowship, perfect union for eternity. From the moment of the resurrection/rapture onward, Paul tells us, *"And so we will be with the Lord forever*. Therefore encourage one another with these words"* (1 Thessalonians 4:17-18).

Even with the epic events of the rapture, receiving rewards, and the union of Christ and the church, there is still much more to come in our future heavenly journey. Just as we catch our glorified-spiritual-body's breath, we will experience another one-time event that is reserved only for angels and the church!

CHAPTER 7

Saddle Your Horses

The armies of heaven were following him, riding on white horses and dressed in fine linen, white and clean.

REVELATION 19:14

The horses snorted as our band of explorers emerged from the cool shadow of the woods. Hooves were still wet from carrying human cargo across trails and creek beds. Riders' thighs were a little sore from the irregular bumping and shifting caused by steep inclines and equally as steep descents. But as the trail opened into a lush field and the warm sun and comfortable breeze landed upon us, both equine and human excitement rose to the fore. It was time.

Gentle kicks from boots in stirrups, coupled with sharp voice commands, set the horses racing. The awkward swaying walk turned into an uncomfortable, bumpy trot. But soon the quickening pace transitioned into long, smooth strides as the horses peaked into full gallop.

As our heart rates increased and our grips tightened around the weathered leather straps, we stood with the balls of our feet pressed hard against the metal bar at the bottom of the stirrups. We leaned forward, intuitively shifting our weight low as the horses kicked their hooves against the ground, and then we would drift slightly upward when the horses would glide through the air weightless before gracefully touching down. The audible thunder of the hoofbeats beneath us paused for a split second as each horse would go airborne again and again. Our adrenaline rushed as the speed increased. A sense of excitement—mixed with a bit of healthy fear—flooded our minds. The power of these magnificent creatures reverberated so closely under us as we raced across the wide-open expanse.

Although I grew up in the suburbs of Washington, DC, as a teenager I had a few opportunities to go outside of the city and ride horses. Some occasions were set trail rides, but my favorite horse-riding experiences were those where we had free rein to explore wooded trails, meandering creeks, and open fields where the horses could gallop.

Trail rides are fun, but a few hours of climbing and descending hills, trotting over bumpy ground, and enduring the constant shifting of your body's weight and balance while on the back of a horse can wear out the rider that hasn't been conditioned for long trail rides. In contrast, open fields where horses can gallop freely provide a completely different experience. It is almost as if the stalwart steeds were created for that very task.

If you are a believer in Christ and you have never ridden a horse, you will get your chance. After the heavenly experiences described in the previous chapters, you will have the single most amazing ride in history as we return with Christ on air-gliding horses. Perhaps you didn't realize this was in store for your future. Allow me to explain.

Perspective Is Key

If you have ever studied eschatology (the study of last things), perhaps you have seen artistic renderings of the return of Christ on a white horse. These artistic depictions are usually shown from the point of view of people standing on earth, looking up at the amazing sight as the glory of the heavenly dimension bursts through the space-time continuum, and the unseen realm invades the atmosphere of the earth. In truth, this is not the point of view that you will want to have when this amazing event occurs.

The perspective that believers will have will be from the reverse angle. Rather than witnessing Christ from below descending from heaven to earth, believers in Jesus will be behind him on our own heavenly horses, taking part of the most epic roller-coaster-like descent anyone has ever experienced.

Just such an experience is one reason why we will need new, glorified spiritual bodies suitable for heaven. If you'll recall, we will receive these new bodies at the moment of the rapture. Our current physiology simply could not handle the experiences of heaven. Just as astronauts need space suits to withstand the conditions of space, we will need (and thankfully will receive) new bodies fit for heaven and built for eternity.

The Adventure Begins

Every newly married couple dreams of living an adventure together. It is hardwired into our psyche. Unfortunately, our entire experience in the natural world is marred by sin—degraded by the fall and vandalized by the initial rebellion. Yet even in a fallen world, the beauty of marriage still shines through. It really can be a thrilling journey that glorifies God and blesses others. This picture points to an ultimate reality, our new life with Christ, which is an eternal adventure.

Following the bema seat and the wedding ceremony, the next event on the heavenly agenda is the beginning of the marriage adventure that is—quite ironically—a return to earth. While we will have been experiencing the glories of heaven after the rapture, the earth will be going through the seven-year tribulation period, building up to the moment of Christ's return at the end of this horrific time of God's wrath being unleashed on the planet.

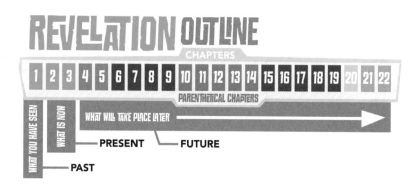

At last, in the closing throes of the tribulation, with the earth completely ravaged and the sun, moon, and stars blacked out from preceding judgments, the blazing glory of the Lord will pierce the sky as Jesus leads the armies of heaven into the earthly realm. Heaven and earth will begin to collide.

The armies of the world will be gathered for what they think is a war against God, but little will they realize that they are preparing themselves as a macabre feast for flesh-eating birds. Imagine this scene, and as you do, remember that you will be witnessing it from the perspective of heaven if you are a Christ follower.

In Revelation 19:11-16, John says,

> I saw heaven standing open and there before me was a white horse, whose rider is called Faithful and True. With justice he judges and wages war. His eyes are like blazing fire, and on his head are many crowns. He has a name written on him that no one knows but he himself. He is dressed in a robe dipped in blood, and his name is the Word of God. The armies of heaven were following him, riding on white horses and dressed in fine linen, white and clean. Coming out of his mouth is a sharp sword with which to strike down the nations. "He will rule them with an iron scepter." He treads the winepress of the fury of the wrath of God Almighty. On his robe and on his thigh he has this name written: KING OF KINGS AND LORD OF LORDS.

Little baby Jesus. Meek and mild Jesus. Grace-filled Jesus. Suffering, submissive Jesus. Now, at this guaranteed future moment, he will arrive as the most powerful and righteous conqueror history, heaven, or earth has ever seen. He is, simply put, King of kings and Lord of lords! No one else can even compare.

In a careful study of this passage, we see the piercing and all-knowing gaze of the King-Savior's eyes, which blaze like fire. We catch a glimpse of his stack of crowns. He is rightful King of everything on every level. Yet there is still mystery to the King, who has an unknown name written on him. Perhaps we will have the privilege of learning this new name upon his return.

Additionally, in the ancient world, to know someone's name meant to have an advantage over them. Jesus is King of the hill. The enemy will have no actual or apparent advantage over him. At the cross, the enemy had an advantage (or so he thought). He leveraged sinful humanity to kill the Savior. But at Christ's return there will be no angle, no advantage, no hidden plot, no secret weapon. All will be laid bare, and our Savior-King will obliterate evil and claim his victory. Aside from one last attempted coup (which we'll discuss in the next chapter), the long-awaited judgment will have finally come.

Hence the blood on the robe of the Warrior-King. This is not the shed blood of the Savior, but the trampled blood of enemies. The necessary opposite side of the grace coin is judgment. God's wrath must be satisfied if he is just. Evil must be punished if God is righteous. Jesus satisfied God's justice on the cross, but most will reject this payment and—sadly—have to pay for it on their own.

At the end of the tribulation period, the armies of the antichrist will have chosen to be on his side, and will literally try to fight God. How tragic that people can be so deceived. We'll discuss more about God's justice in chapter 12 when we discuss the doctrine of hell.

But as we see in Revelation 19, the armies of heaven (notice the plural here) will return with Christ to witness his victory. The armies of heaven include the church-age believers who have their glorified bodies and wedding clothes. They also includes the angelic armies. Many passages cite that angels will accompany Christ at his return (Matthew 13:41; 16:27; 24:30-31; Mark 8:38; Luke 9:26; 2 Thessalonians 1:7).

The Dinner Party You Want to Avoid

In Revelation 19:17-21, we read,

> And I saw an angel standing in the sun, who cried in a loud voice to all the birds flying in midair, "Come, gather together for the great supper of God, so that you may eat the flesh of kings, generals, and the mighty, of horses and their riders, and the flesh of all people, free and slave, great and small."
>
> Then I saw the beast and the kings of the earth and their armies gathered together to wage war against the rider on the horse and his army. But the beast was captured, and with it the false prophet who had performed the signs on its behalf. With these signs he had deluded those who had received the mark of the beast and worshiped its image. The two of them were thrown alive into the fiery lake of burning sulfur. The rest were killed with the sword coming out of the mouth of the rider on the horse, and all the birds gorged themselves on their flesh.

Now there's a scene you'll never see illustrated in a children's picture book Bible! In many of the modern Christian resources produced today, certain aspects of the Bible have been toned down (sometimes understandably so). But the truth is, there are many narratives in Scripture that would be rated R if were they made into movies. Revelation is definitely one of those narratives. Just here in chapter 19, we see Warrior-King Jesus slaughtering the evil armies of the world with simply his words.

Following the army-destroying shockwaves of Jesus' fatal voice, we are given a picture of a horrific scene that would make Alfred Hitchcock's classic film *The Birds* look like a preschool show. Bloody, flesh-eating birds feasting on the fallen armies of the world are the complete opposite of the glorious white-linen wedding supper in heaven. The contrast is stark, vivid, and very intentional. Mercy has run its course. Grace is all used up. It will be time for evil to meet its deserved punishment.

Heavenly Connection

You may read this chapter and wonder why it is included in a book about heaven. Simply put, heaven is the result of our salvation, and the return of Christ is a foundational and essential component of our salvation. The church at large often focuses on the cross and the victory of the resurrection—and rightfully so. But often what is omitted is the return of Christ to execute that victory.

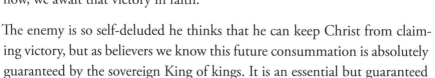

We have an empty cross and an empty tomb to look back on. We also have an occupied throne to look up to in the present. And we have a future event to look forward to, when Christ will return to claim the victory. Right now, we await that victory in faith.

The enemy is so self-deluded he thinks that he can keep Christ from claiming victory, but as believers we know this future consummation is absolutely guaranteed by the sovereign King of kings. It is an essential but guaranteed component of our ability to spend eternity with God in heaven. So there is a direct and foundational connection between eschatology and the doctrine of heaven.

Remember, heaven is intermediate at the moment. There is a necessary process in motion to bring heaven and earth into the same environment once again. The return of Christ is a part of this process that will bring us to the absolute apex of history! Turn the page and discover the era that supersedes all other earthly epochs—and your future heavenly role in it. Your supernatural horse ride will just be the beginning!

CHAPTER 8

The Heavenly High Point of History

This, then, is how you should pray: "Our Father in heaven, hallowed be your name, your kingdom come, your will be done, on earth as it is in heaven."

MATTHEW 6:9-10

Have you ever thought deeply about that verse as you have prayed it? Myriads of Christians have prayed that prayer—perhaps billions of times. To use the poetic and well-known rendering the Christian church has corporately prayed, "Thy kingdom come. Thy will be done, on earth as it is in heaven." The church has prayed this in many languages for nearly 2,000 years. God will one day answer this prayer. It has yet to be fulfilled, as there has never been a time when God's complete will has been done "on earth as it is in heaven." That phrase means complete sovereign rule.

THY KINGDOM COME

There is a future time period that comes prior to the eternal state that supersedes all other earthly epochs. It is the climax of history and the end of a long chain of mankind's failed attempts to extend God's rule properly.

If you are familiar with my books, you may recall that I love story, film, and animation. There's an old adage in the film industry—particularly in animation—that goes, "Story is king." As human beings we resonate with story, and I believe the key reason this is true is that we are image bearers of the divine Storyteller.

While each historical account in Scripture works as its own stand-alone story—complete with setup, conflict, and resolution—the entire canon of the Bible cohesively unites into one grand narrative. Now by story, I do not mean to imply that it is fictional. Quite the contrary. Scripture is 100 percent accurate and the most trustworthy book ever written.

Creation was a literal event. The flood of Noah's day was a literal event. The Israelites' exodus, wandering, and entrance into the promised land really occurred. The coming of Christ, the work of the cross, the resurrection, and the birth and growth of the church as detailed in the book of Acts were all literal historical events. Internal and external manuscript evidence support Scripture. Archeology supports it. Hundreds of fulfilled prophecies support it. And contrary to common secular belief, even science supports the accuracy of Scripture.

But the Bible is not merely a textbook full of data. It is not solely a history book or a science book (though it is historically and scientifically accurate). The connective tissue of the Bible is story. Within that story, there are very clear epochs or eras—undeniable historical markers that delineate between certain time periods where God worked a little differently in each era.

For example, when you read the pages of Genesis, it is very clear that the time period of creation before the fall was very different to what it was after the fall. Similarly, the time period before the flood was very different than the time period after the flood. The time period during the Mosaic law was different than the time period we're now in, the church age. The current condition of the earth is clearly different than what the future eternal state will be. You get the picture. It is important to note that the means of salvation never changes, just the manner in which God tasks humanity to extend his rule or implement his plan shifts.

The apostle Paul refers to a couple of these eras, or time periods, in Ephesians 3:2-5. He wrote,

> Surely you have heard about the administration of God's grace that was given to me for you, that is, the mystery made known to me by revelation, as I have already written briefly. In reading this, then, you will be able to understand my insight into the mystery of Christ, which was not made known to people in other generations as it has now been revealed by the Spirit to God's holy apostles and prophets.

The word Paul used in Ephesians 3:2 translated "administration" is the Greek word *oikonomia*, which is used nine times in the New Testament. Depending on the translation of the Bible you are reading, the word is translated as administration, economy, stewardship, management, or dispensation. In each era, God tasks his image bearers with an updated version of extending his rule. In each era, the human effort has failed. In the final administration, God will extend his rule via the millennial kingdom. He will come and do it himself. This future golden age will truly be the heavenly high point of history!

So let's review how God has tasked mankind through the ages in a bit more detail. God's initial command to Adam and Eve was to "be fruitful and increase in number; fill the earth and subdue it" (Genesis 1:28). In more understandable terms, God was giving the task of extending his rule over the whole earth to Adam and Eve, his image bearers. But they failed by disobeying God's command, and sin entered the scene. Despite this foul-up, the task to extend God's rule remained, and over and over again, humans failed to complete the task.

God even chose a unique people for himself, the descendants of Abraham through the promised son Isaac. They were to display his rule and extend it

to the whole earth, but they failed as well. Then Christ came to redeem mankind, and when he returned to heaven the church was born. The intended purpose of the church was to do the same thing—to extend God's rule and bear his image uniquely during a specific time period. But Scripture informs us that the church will ultimately also fail at this task.

So the biblical narrative is the overarching story of different eras during which God's people were tasked with extending his rule but failed. During each era, God gave light, but each one has ended in darkness and failure. After the end of the church age (as we've alluded to in previous chapters), an evil global leader will arrive on the scene who will deceive the world into worshipping a false God, and the world will literally and figuratively go dark.

Then the heavenly light-piercing moment described in the previous chapter will take place when Christ returns, destroys the enemy, and initiates God's kingdom on earth. God's image bearers will have failed in each previous era, showing that God must fully intervene and do it himself. Only the holy, sinless, and almighty Savior can extend his rule to the whole earth. One day the original charge to Adam will be completed through the Second Adam (1 Corinthians 15:45-49).

God's Good Global Government

That subheading is a bit of a tongue twister, but each word is intentional. As opposed to the various human attempts to establish a global government—by the likes of Nimrod (Tower of Babel), modern despots such as

Hitler, or the future evil antichrist (who will achieve this feat as a global dictator)—God will have the last word and will usher in the true version of a utopian kingdom age. God's rule will reign. It will therefore be truly good. It will be global. And it will be a literal government, not an allegorical reign through the advancing church, as some theologians assert.

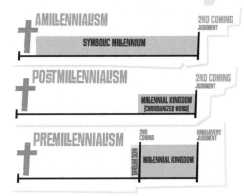

There are three views of the kingdom age that people hold to (see chart), but the only one that fits the specific prophecies given in the Old Testament without abusing the clear language of the various passages is the premillennial view. Premillennialism holds to the view that Christ will return prior to ("pre") a literal future kingdom age.

There are many specific Old Testament prophecies about a descendant of David who will rule the world from Jerusalem. These repeated prophecies—which specifically address what the world's people, animals, topography, and government will be like during the future kingdom age—have yet to be fulfilled. The details included in these prophesies are too overarching and specific to be turned into mere allegory.

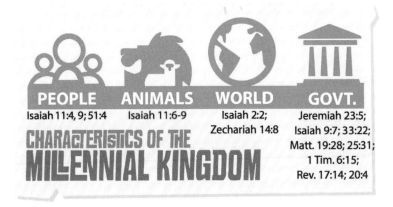

Without going too far down the rabbit hole, consider this familiar verse often associated with Christmas. In Isaiah 9:6, we read, "For to us a child is born, to us a son is given, and the government will be on his shoulders. And he will be called Wonderful Counselor, Mighty God, Everlasting Father, Prince of Peace."

People readily accept the first phrase is referring to the birth of Christ, hence it is emphasized at Christmastime. The second phrase, a son is given, is understood to be Christ's work on the cross, a la John 3:16. But many people ignore the conclusion of the verse that clearly states that the government will be on his shoulders. That is a direct allusion to the kingdom age, when the long-awaited descendant of David will rule from Jerusalem.

If there is any doubt, check out the next verse in that passage. In Isaiah 9:7, we read, "Of the greatness of his government and peace there will be no end. He will reign on David's throne and over his kingdom, establishing and upholding it with justice and righteousness from that time on and forever."

I've mentioned the millennial kingdom a lot in previous chapters, but now we get to look at it in detail. So what is the millennium (millennial kingdom)? The millennium is a future 1,000-year period that begins after Christ's return to earth at the end of the tribulation. During this time, Satan will be bound in what is known as the abyss, or pit. And Christ will establish his perfect kingdom on earth, ruling from Jerusalem. The resurrected and raptured church will assist Jesus in ruling the world.

REVELATION 20:2-7
1000 YEARS | 6X
(1X IN EACH VERSE)

The purposes of this period are (1) to fulfill God's Old Testament promises for the future kingdom of Israel, which will have a ruler from the line of David, and (2) to demonstrate that even in a perfect world with a perfect ruler, mankind will still choose to rebel against God. This will be clearly demonstrated when Satan is let loose at the end of the millennium for one last battle. He will be given the opportunity to convince people of the world to join him in one last rebellion against God. Many will choose to do so. After this final battle, Satan will be defeated and cast into the lake of fire, where he will remain forever (Revelation 20:7-10).

It is my firm belief that the millennium is a future, literal 1,000-year period. And as it pertains to our subject of heaven in this book, the most relevant detail about the future kingdom is that church-age believers (that's you and me), along with Old Testament saints and tribulation saints, will rule and reign with Christ in it (see Revelation 1:6; 5:10). Two of Jesus' parables—the bags of gold (Matthew 25:14-30) and the ten minas (Luke 19:11-27)—give us further insight into the principles of the kingdom, and some of the rewards or privileges believers will have in it.

Life in the Millennial Kingdom

We do not know all of the details about what we will be doing in the future kingdom, but we do gain some insight from Scripture. We have previously looked at and gained some insight from the parable of the bags of gold from Matthew 25. In the parable of the minas in Luke 19, Jesus also ties the parable's theme directly to the kingdom age. Jesus had just finished his encounter with Zacchaeus in Jericho and was on his way to Jerusalem. Luke 19:11 says, "He went on to tell them a parable, because he was near Jerusalem and the people thought that the kingdom of God was going to appear at once."

I'LL BE BACK.

Jesus launches into telling the crowd the parable by first setting the scene. In verses 12-13, Jesus said, "A man of noble birth went to a distant country to have himself appointed king and then to return. So he called ten of his servants and gave them ten minas. 'Put this money to work,' he said, 'until I come back.'"

I have witnessed many people overlook those opening verses, but those introductory words are important. They lay out Jesus' clear indication that the kingdom age is not the current age, during which we are managing his affairs—preaching the gospel and awaiting his return. The kingdom age is a future time period that takes place after his return. According to this parable, those who work to accomplish the king's will while he is away will be placed in charge of cities in the future kingdom—proportional to how they leveraged what thy had been given originally. Remember our bema seat discussion from chapter 5?

So in the millennial kingdom, we will be given some type of oversight over a portion of the kingdom. As referenced above, we will rule and reign with Christ. Keep in mind that God always pairs our calling and responsibilities with our individual personality. In this life, our spiritual gifts, talents, abilities, passions, interests, personality traits, and experiences all play into discovering our calling. This will not be lost in the future kingdom.

We see in Scripture that when Jesus was in his glorified body after the resurrection, people recognized him (with the exception of when he purposefully hid his identity on the road to Emmaus in Luke 24). He could also eat; Jesus was physical, yet he could travel at the speed of thought and enter rooms without using the door (Luke 24:30-31, 36-43).

At the Mount of Transfiguration, when Peter, James, and John saw Jesus glorified along with Moses and Elijah, they knew who Moses and Elijah were without ever having met them before (Matthew 17:1-13; Mark 9:2-13; Luke

9:28-36). In our glorified state we will know who people are, and their personalities, purpose, and calling will remain intact.

Here's a mind-blowing fact: When we are raptured and receive our glorified bodies, we will be able to do the same things as Jesus did in his glorified body. In 1 John 3:2, we read, "Dear friends, now we are children of God, and what we will be has not yet been made known. But we know that when Christ appears, we shall be like him, for we shall see him as he is." We will be physical but also supernatural. We will be able to travel at the speed of thought. We will be able to enjoy food (thank you, Lord). Best of all, we will no longer have a sin nature or be subject to its curse.

RAPTURE

Right now, our daily lives are so thoroughly impacted by the effects of the curse and our sin nature (or what is referred to as "the flesh") that we can't even envision life without them. Imagine being able to serve the Lord to perfection. If you are a believer in Christ, that will be the case for you during the kingdom age, and you are preparing for it today.

All of that to say, what we do now matters more than we realize. We're not merely making a living and just trying to get through life in order to arrive safely at death. We are preparing for our work in the millennial kingdom and beyond! How's that for adding value to your daily grind? In some manner, each of us will have responsibilities in the kingdom that fit who we are. It will not be drudgery. It will be the most exhilarating, fulfilling, and rewarding work we ever do. And this concept of work will extend into eternity (but more on that later).

Here are a few more things we will be doing in the future kingdom age: We will judge (1 Corinthians 6:2). We will have authority over the nations (Revelation 2:26-27). We will also be teachers. Recall that those who will reside on the earth include believers who survived the tribulation and are not yet in a glorified state. As new generations of people are born, we will again be Christ's witnesses as we help to fill the earth with the knowledge of the Lord (Habakkuk 2:14). Lastly, we will witness the final demise of Satan (Revelation 20:7-10).

The Overture to Eternity

But wait, there's more! Unlike a cheesy infomercial attempting to sell you some multiuse product in four easy payments, I really mean it. There is so much more to come that lies beyond the future kingdom age. The millennial kingdom is merely the front porch of eternity, an overture of sorts.

The overture is an orchestral arrangement played at the beginning of a musical drama. It contains abbreviated sections and variations of the musical pieces that will be heard throughout the performance to come. It is the coming-attraction teaser trailer to the big blockbuster. The introduction to the main event. The prelude to the full masterpiece.

Similarly, the millennial kingdom will be a taste of what is to come. A thousand years is just a drop in the ocean of eternity, and our good heavenly Father saves the best for last! If this has you intrigued, then let's continue on in our chronological journey of events. We have toured the intermediate state of heaven and finished our discussion about the overture to heaven. Now on to our last stop—our future with God in heaven's final and eternal state.

CHAPTER 9

The Master Restorer

See, I will create new heavens and a new earth. The former things will not be remembered, nor will they come to mind.

ISAIAH 65:17

A friend of mine used to own a few classic cars. One of them was a restored 1966 Shelby GT350 Mustang. If you've seen the movie *Ford v Ferrari*, you will be familiar with the backstory of the Shelby pedigree. Carroll Shelby developed and manufactured performance vehicles and was brought on to the Ford racing team to help produce a car that could beat the dominant Ferrari racing team at the 24 Hours of Le Mans race in France—an effort in which they succeeded with the Ford GT40 in 1966. So my friend's former car is from the same model year as the much-celebrated Ford victory over Ferrari.

A classic car like that is rare. The total number of 1966 Shelby GT350 Mustangs produced was 2,386.[9] Low production counts are one reason why classic cars are rare, but there is another contributing factor that affects all classic cars that makes them even more so today—decay.

I touched on this earlier in the book, but we often overlook many of the consequences of mankind's fall into sin. One of them is decay. Or in modern scientific terms, the second law of thermodynamics, known as the law of increasing entropy. This universal law highlights the fact that everything in a closed system will wear out, run out of energy, and break down. The universe is dying a slow energy death as time goes on.

By the way, this shows that everything in the universe had a beginning, just as stated in Genesis 1. Since the fall, the curse of sin—which leads to death—has affected the universe—from stars to subatomic particles and everything in between. People age. Disease spreads. DNA degrades. And classic cars rust and wear out. The second law of thermodynamics essentially catalogues the scientific observation of the curse.

But in the world of classic cars there is another force at work, the classic car restorer. These are people who have the passion, knowledge, connections, training, and equipment to recondition rusting and worn-out cars to their original pristine beauty and functionality.

Great lengths are taken to track down original parts for anything that is missing or ruined. Classic car restorers will search high and low to find just the right component from the manufacturing year of the car. If that is not possible, they create new parts that fit the exact specifications of the original. By the time these wizards of refurbishment are finished, they deliver completely restored classic cars that are so perfect you would think you stepped back in time to see the moment the car first rolled out of the factory.

God is the great cosmic restorer. The Bible details the four-part story of creation, fall, redemption, and restoration. In chapter 2, I encouraged you to take some time to read Genesis 1–2, followed by Revelation 21–22. If you took me up on that prompt, what you probably noticed is that God's will is always accomplished and that he is a God of restoration.

God restores the lives of people through salvation and sanctification (spiritual growth). He rebuilds relationships. He creates unity where it didn't exist prior. He brings light to darkness, hope to the hopeless, joy to the downtrodden, peace to conflict, and a right standing with him when there is seemingly no possible way for reconciliation.

In the case of creation and the fall, God will restore heaven and earth to their rightful condition. One day, yet-future heaven and earth will once again unite as one. God will enable a revised and better version of Eden, where he will dwell with humankind in a sinless and perfect environment. This has been promised in both the Old and New Testaments. In addition to the verse at the opening of this chapter (Isaiah 65:17), consider these two verses:

> Isaiah 66:22—"'As the new heavens and the new earth that I make will endure before me,' declares the LORD, 'so will your name and descendants endure.'"
>
> 2 Peter 3:13—"In keeping with his promise we are looking forward to a new heaven and a new earth, where righteousness dwells."

Before we unpack the details about the new heavens and the new earth, there is one final event to survey. God will wrap up one final matter ahead of when the current intermediate state of heaven is converted into its final and eternal form.

The Final Event of History

In the previous chapter we discussed the millennial kingdom, the heavenly high point of history. Following that will come one more item of business as time as we know it concludes—before we enter the eternal state that is outside of time and will never end. This future key event is the final judgment. This end-of-time judgment will be strictly for unbelievers, and it is known as the great white throne judgment. (Remember, Christians will have stood before the judgment seat of Christ [bema] to have our works evaluated for reward. Believers' sins were dealt with at the cross.) So after 1,000 years of the millennial kingdom, the final rebellion, and Satan's ultimate judgment, we read about a future occasion when all unbelievers will stand before God to answer for their sins.

We read about this event in Revelation 20:11-15, where John describes what he saw with these words:

> I saw a great white throne and him who was seated on it. The earth and the heavens fled from his presence, and there was no place for them. And I saw the dead, great and small, standing before the throne, and books were opened. Another book was opened,

which is the book of life. The dead were judged according to what they had done as recorded in the books. The sea gave up the dead that were in it, and death and Hades gave up the dead that were in them, and each person was judged according to what they had done. Then death and Hades were thrown into the lake of fire. The lake of fire is the second death. Anyone whose name was not found written in the book of life was thrown into the lake of fire.

In this amazing scene we see everything literally fade away except the throne and the books. Are these literal books or some kind of heavenly databank? The instances of the words "book" and "books" used here in this passage come from the Greek root word *biblos* (βίβλος), and they refer to a scroll, book, or volume. The books are a divinely kept volume of data on each person who has ever lived. If you think the datacenters that governments and transnational data companies have and maintain are large, just think about the amount of data God has kept over the centuries. Every thought, action, motive, and word of every person who has ever existed or will exist is logged in God's supernatural library of "books."

Notice also that John mentions that the lake of fire is the second death. In Scripture, we learn that there are two births and two deaths. We experience a natural birth when we are physically born. And there is a second spiritual birth if we accept Christ (John 3:3-6). We have a natural death when our current physical bodies die. And there is a second spiritual death, which John refers to here as the lake of fire (Revelation 20:14). So the implication being: If you are born twice, you will only die once; but if you are born only once, you will die twice.

The End of History[10]

The eternal state is the final condition of the universe after all is said and done. After the rapture, tribulation, millennial kingdom, and great white throne judgment, Scripture tells us the old heaven and earth will be dissolved and a new heaven and earth will be created in absolute perfection and will last for eternity. Revelation 21–22 provides us with an amazing description of this final state. There will be no sorrow, no sin, no suffering, no pain, no death, and no evil. We will enjoy unending and perfect unity with Christ and experience the fullness of his blessings. This final condition in which we will live is beyond description.

John did his best throughout Revelation to describe what he saw and experienced. He had a front-row seat to the heavenly and supernatural, to technology that was millennia beyond anything he'd ever seen, and destruction on a level that nobody other than God had previously known. The judgments of the tribulation period were difficult for John to describe. Next, his description of the millennial kingdom posed an entirely new challenge to explanation. Then in writing Revelation 21–22, John had the ultimate task of describing the eternal state—the final condition of all things.

I find it interesting that in Revelation, John used 16 chapters to describe the seven-year tribulation period, but only one chapter for the 1,000-year millennial kingdom and one chapter for the eternal state, which will last forever. I believe a reason for this is that John simply could not adequately describe what he saw, nor could he fully comprehend it.

The eternal state will be so otherworldly that most of its attributes are beyond description. It's not a stretch to imagine that there will be colors, sights, sounds, smells, physics, and experiences that we can't currently comprehend with our limited thinking and in our mortal bodies.

In 2 Corinthians 12:4, Paul describes a time when he was "caught up" to the third heaven and witnessed things that were so glorious, so amazing, so mind-blowing that he was not even allowed to share what he witnessed! Earlier, in his first letter to the Corinthians, Paul referenced the prophet Isaiah when he wrote, "Eye has not seen, nor ear heard, nor have entered into the heart of man the things which God has prepared for those who love Him" (1 Corinthians 2:9 NKJV).

In Revelation 21, rather than attempt to explain everything he experienced, John spends more time describing what will not be present in the eternal state. No more death. No more pain. No more suffering. No more tears. No more relational breakdown. We also find there will be no sea. Seas separate people. Any type of separation will be a thing of the past. Every race, tribe, tongue, and people group will live in perfect unity and perfect community with each other and with the Lord.

Heaven is mentioned around 532 times in the Bible, and more than 10 percent of those occurrences are in the book of Revelation! John speaks of heaven in no less than 55 instances. It is a real place, in an unseen realm, outside of our space-time continuum. But it is not ethereal. Humans do not become one with the universe or float around as wispy, bodiless spirits. We will maintain our identity. We will still have the glorified spiritual bodies that we received at the rapture. We will still be us, only much better, and we will be living in perfect unity with God and others. I'm sure if we caught a glimpse of what Paul or John saw, we too would be short on words.

A New Jerusalem—the Eternal Capital City

The crowning feature of the new heavens and the new earth will be its capital city, the new Jerusalem. Revelation 21 describes the heavenly Jerusalem coming down from God. This heavenly Jerusalem might already exist now. Jesus may have been talking about this city when he told his disciples that he was going away to make a dwelling place for each of his followers (John 14:2).

QUICK FACT: DID YOU KNOW...

that God is building a custom designed mansion for you if you are his?

Throughout the Bible, Jerusalem has played a key role in God's unfolding story. It only makes sense that this important city—the one that herniates the backs of those who try to move its borders (Zechariah 12:3) and the one

that God calls the apple of his own eye (Zechariah 2:8)—would receive such immense glory and attention in the eternal state along with the new heaven and the new earth.

Scripture speaks of Jerusalem as the center of the nations. Indeed, it is the historical crossroads of Europe, Asia, and Africa. As an interesting aside, many written languages that originate to the east of Jerusalem are read right to left, while most written languages that originate to the west of Jerusalem read from left to right. Both trade routes and languages all seem to point to Jerusalem. Often, when Scripture cites a cardinal direction (north, south, east, or west) it is in relation to Jerusalem.

In addition to being the geographical and linguistic center of the world, Jerusalem has been at the center of at least 36 wars. And it is considered the epicenter of Bible prophecy. The destruction of Jerusalem in AD 70 was prophesied by Daniel (Daniel 9) and by Jesus in the Olivet Discourse (Matthew 24; Mark 13; Luke 21). Luke 21:24 informs us that Jerusalem would remain out of the hands of the Jewish people "until the times of the Gentiles are fulfilled." This is significant.

In 1948, Israel became a nation again in a single day (exactly as foretold in Isaiah 66:8). Later, in 1967, Israel once again gained control of Jerusalem as a result of the Six-Day War. The nations of the world (via the United Nations) are obsessed with both Israel and Jerusalem, just as prophesied in Zechariah 12:3. Apparently, the times of the Gentiles are transitioning to set the stage for all end-times events to take place.

This central location theme of Bible prophecy finds its full and final resolution in Revelation. John provides the first of several details about the new

Jerusalem in Revelation 21:2, where he wrote: "I saw the Holy City, the new Jerusalem, coming down out of heaven from God, prepared as a bride beautifully dressed for her husband." Then, John specifies several more features about the city in verses 9-27, and some final elements in Revelation 22:1-5.

The most descriptive portion is found in 21:16-21, yet I highly recommend you carefully and slowly read the entire chapter for context. John describes the new Jerusalem as a cube, approximately 1,400 miles in each dimension, coming from heaven to earth in glorious fashion. To give you an idea of its size, this immense city is slightly smaller than our moon, it would stretch from Florida to Maine, and it would be 150,000 times the size of London. Will this city rest on earth? Will it hover? Will it orbit the earth? We are not told, but one day we will find out.

Notice that the city will exist prior to the eternal state. It comes down and is presented. Other passages of Scripture provide hints about the new Jerusalem, and (as I mentioned above) many Bible teachers believe it already exists and is what Jesus was referring to in John 14:2 when he said, "My Father's house has many rooms; if that were not so, would I have told you that I am going there to prepare a place for you?"

The new Jerusalem is also the city of promise that is spoken of in the book of Hebrews. In Hebrews 11:10, concerning Abraham's faith in his future inheritance, we read, "He was looking forward to the city with foundations, whose architect and builder is God." Then later, the writer of Hebrews reminds and encourages believers, "Here we do not have an enduring city, but we are looking for the city that is to come" (13:14).

FACTS ABOUT THE NEW JERUSALEM

- Height x Width x Depth—1,380 miles in each direction.

- Cube vs. Pyramid—Pyramids are associated with the occult and sun worship. Cubes are associated with God's presence in the temple/Holy of Holies.

- Resurrected bodies are not subject to gravity—"Streets" may include vertical passageways.

- City "blocks" may be cubes as well—The city will fit how our resurrected bodies function

- The new Jerusalem could house 20 billion people—even at this number, it would provide an average of 75 acres for each person and still utilize only 25 percent of the total area of the city.[11]

Jesus has been building this city for nearly 2,000 years, adding "mansions" (as some translations render John 14:2) for each person who accepts Christ. If he created the universe in six days, we can only imagine what the new Jerusalem will be like given that it is two millennia in the making!

In Revelation 21–22, we learn that this city of God will be covered in jewels and precious stones of every kind, purer than anything we've ever seen. God will have his throne there, and his glory will be the source of the city's never-ending light. In Scripture, God's presence is often described as brilliant light. In the new Jerusalem, the glory of God's presence will burst forth in unlimited radiating brilliance, reflecting throughout the jeweled heavenly city in a dazzling display of refracting color.

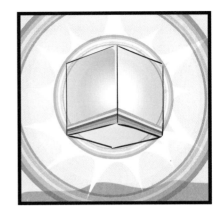

The city will have 12 gates, each made of a single pearl and eternally linked to the 12 tribes of Israel. The new Jerusalem will also be built on 12 solid foundations, eternally linked to and named after the apostles, whom we are told are the foundation of the church (Ephesians 2:20). The makeup of the city will be a constant reminder of the unity between Old and New Testament saints of every tribe, nation, tongue, and people. It will be characterized by complete harmony and perfect God-honoring community.

Heaven's "main street" will be made of pure gold and a river will flow from the throne room of God right down the middle of the street. Angels will stand at the gates, and the city will be populated by God's redeemed children. The new Jerusalem—the capital city of eternity—will be the perpetual reminder of God's redemptive plan, the plan he perfectly carried out through the ages. And we will call this place home.

Recreated or Restored?

As I highlighted at the opening of this chapter, God is in the business of restoration. He does not destroy what was marred by sin; rather, he restores it by getting rid of the sin and the effects of the fall. In 2 Peter 3:10, we read, "The heavens will disappear with a roar; the elements will be destroyed by fire, and the earth and everything done in it will be laid bare."

Destroyed but not annihilated. Laid bare but not done away with. Theologians vary on their views of whether God will completely recreate the heavens and earth, or instead, redeem what he already created. I hold to the view that God will use the same material he originally created to form the new heavens and the new earth, but he will burn all corruption out of it. He will purge it from anything affected by original sin and the effects of the fall. At the rapture, God will resurrect the original bodies of believers (1 Thessalonians 4:16) and give them glorified bodies. With the new heavens and the new earth, I believe God will resurrect (so to speak) his original creation to make it into a new glorified form. This fits God's character and his pattern of action.

That should be extremely encouraging to us as believers. God doesn't waste anything. He doesn't throw out what he has created. He is the Master Restorer. What he creates is good. And the Lord is in the business of restoring lives, relationships, and even creation itself to their original intended purpose and condition, and as we saw in this chapter, with some exciting upgrades too!

SECTION 3:

COMMON QUESTIONS ABOUT HEAVEN

CHAPTER 10

Who Is Going and Who Is Not?

I am the gate; whoever enters through me will be saved. They will come in and go out, and find pasture.

JOHN 10:9

I've been out of the country a few times and have discovered there is one all-important item you need to have when traveling overseas—a passport. The key request you will hear when checking in for an international flight is, "May I see your passport?" If you cannot supply a valid passport, you will not be getting on the plane.

You can argue your case. You can ask a friend or family member to vouch for you. You can tell the airport staff that you were intending to get your passport before your trip, or you can explain that you have a passport but forgot to bring it. You can show them your other credentials, such as your driver's license or your birth certificate.

You can share your accomplishments, degrees, memberships, or any other accolades with them. You can tell them about your important position in the community or about your life-saving medical training. However, if you don't have your passport, none of that matters. And when it comes to the passport for heaven, it is sinless perfection.

A God of Wrath?

Because we currently live during a time before the eternal state, throughout this book I've been cataloging the transition from this world to eternity chronologically. In the previous chapter, I highlighted the final eternal state and the event known as the great white throne judgment that will precede it. We have also already discussed the church-age believer's judgment (for rewards, not admission to heaven) that will take place at the bema seat, which is also known as the judgment seat of Christ.

There are other judgments that will occur as well, including the judgment of the nations (known as the sheep and goats judgment) that will take place after the tribulation and before the millennial kingdom (see Matthew 25:31-46). In this judgment, God will consider how individuals treated the Jewish people during the tribulation period. Scripture also indicates that at some point (and in some fashion), church-age believers will judge the angels (1 Corinthians 6:2-3).

As we consider those future judgments, we are reminded of the judgments of the past. As recorded in Scripture, these judgments include the consequences of the fall (Genesis 3:14-24), the judgment of the global flood of Noah's day (Genesis 7:17-24), the judgment of the Tower of Babel (Genesis 11:5-9), the judgment of Sodom and Gomorrah (Genesis 19:1-29), the judgment of Pharaoh and Egypt's false gods (Exodus 7–12), the judgment of ancient Israel (2 Kings 17:22-23) and Judah (2 Kings 25:1-21), and finally—thankfully—the judgment of sin for all who would believe in Christ (Isaiah 53:4-8; John 3:16-17).

So our multifaceted God is, among many other things, a God of judgment. God's wrath and God's grace are two sides of the same coin. You can't have one without the other. I always grin a bit when I hear someone say something along the lines of, "I like the grace-filled God of the New Testament better than the wrath-filled God of the Old Testament." What an opportunity for a meaningful gospel conversation.

The first thing I want to do is to draw their attention to the book of Revelation. While both grace and wrath are present even in God's judgment (all the way up until someone takes the mark of the beast at the midpoint of the tribulation), Revelation 6–19 details God's active wrath upon the earth. In short, a good God must eventually punish evil. And it is all accomplished for creation's own good.

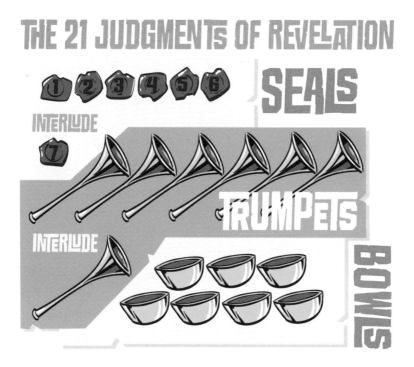

Circling back to the title of this chapter, we ask the question, "Who's going and who's not?" When all is said and done and the merging of heaven and earth is accomplished and the eternal state is firmly established, who is going to be there? What is the essential criterion?

The standard is sinlessness. Only those who are sinless will be there. Only those who have never had an impure thought, motive, or action will be able to stand in the presence of a holy God. Are you feeling nervous yet? So am I. Thankfully, that is not the end of the story. Only those who are sinless will be there—or those to whom sinlessness has been imputed. *Imputed* is a 50-dollar theological word that means someone else's sinless perfection has been credited to us.

That someone else is Jesus. Our accounts were severely overdrawn with no way to pay back the debt, but Jesus paid it all and put us back into right standing with God. Our sin was placed on Christ when he hung on the cross. While Jesus never ceased to be God, somehow—in a way that only God can comprehend—Christ became sin for us (2 Corinthians 5:21). All of God's wrath for all of our sins was placed on Christ. The suffering Jesus endured via flogging, beating, and being nailed to that old rugged cross paled in comparison to the suffering the Son endured when the Father turned from the Son and poured his wrath upon him.

Do You Have Your Passport?

So to answer the question of the title of this chapter: Only those who have placed their trust in the finished work of Christ will be in heaven for eternity. It is our passport. In reference to the verse at the opening of this chapter, John 10:9, this is how we enter the narrow gate. Sadly, those who reject salvation—those who do not have this already-paid-for passport—will not be allowed into heaven. Hell is a tough doctrine, but it is logically and spiritually necessary. We'll discuss hell in more depth in chapter 12, but it is very real, eternal, and one of the two places mankind can spend eternity.

Regarding salvation, the Old Testament saints did not have all of the information about Christ's atoning sacrifice revealed to them; however, they looked forward to God's redeeming work based on what they did know. Genesis 3:15 was the first prophecy of a future Messiah. And many other prophecies followed. People living during the time of the Old Testament didn't have all of the details, but they were responsible for what they knew.

Paul reminds us in Romans 4:3, "What does Scripture say? 'Abraham believed God, and it was credited to him as righteousness.'" Here, Paul is looking back to the promise of an heir that God gave to Abraham in Genesis 15, when God told Abraham (then Abram) that his offspring would compare in number to the stars in the sky. Paul is encouraging believers that it was by Abraham's faith that he was saved, and likewise for the rest of us, accepting God's grace through our faith is what brings us righteousness. God's perfection was credited to Abraham's account based on the future (from Abraham's perspective) work of Christ. Those in the Old Testament looked forward (based on what had been revealed to them), and church-age believers have the privilege of looking backward to the finished work of Christ.

ABRAHAM

If you are reading this, I don't want to assume that you have accepted Christ, and in the case that you haven't, I want to share a bit more about how to have him as your personal Savior. Accepting Christ is not mere mental assent. It is a conscious decision—like what happens on a wedding day. When people get married, they make a commitment. It is an event they can point back to concretely. I don't remember the exact date and time when I accepted Christ at age 13, but I do remember the moment. It was a decision I wrestled with for some months prior to my salvation. I was earnestly seeking truth, and I wanted to believe in Christ if I knew he was for real.

So I began praying that if everything about Christ was truly real, God would simply make me believe in him. I had reasons to believe—fulfilled prophecies and other reasonable evidences—but I still had some doubts. I prayed that God would help me overcome those doubts, and he did. In the middle of praying the same prayer (that God would make me believe if it were all true), a light switch was flipped on in my soul.

I can't explain it fully, but I shifted from praying to believe that Jesus was the Savior to believing he was the Savior, then to asking him to be my personal Savior. I committed to following Jesus (as much as I knew how to at that moment) and concretely nailed down the fact that I was a believer in Christ and had accepted his salvation.

Prior to Christ, we are spiritually dead and under God's wrath. That is not a message you hear preached very often. It is definitely not on the top-ten list of popular Christian T-shirts. But it is true. Once we accept Christ, we come alive spiritually. Scripture refers to this as being born again (John 3:3-6). It is our passport to heaven, so to speak. Do you have yours? If not, please nail that down right now as the Holy Spirit is drawing you. I'll do my best to facilitate.

One does not become a Christian by following a formula, but I've found that what I'm about to share is an effective way to explain what it means to receive Christ and become a true Christian. Some people make the gospel message complex, but it's so uncomplicated a child can understand it. It's as simple as A-B-C.

ADMIT

Admit that you are a sinner. None of us are perfect. We all fall short. Romans 3:23: "All have sinned and fall short of the glory of God." Romans 6:23: "The wages [payment] of sin is death, but the gift of God is eternal life in Christ Jesus our Lord." Coupled with this "admitting" is acknowledging that we agree with God about our sinfulness and our need of a Savior. We do a U-turn in our thinking about sin. Scripture calls this repentance.

BELIEVE

Believe that Jesus is God's Son and that he died on the cross with your sins on him. Believe also that he rose from the dead and is alive forever. God was made flesh and died for us to make a way back to himself. Romans 5:8: "While we were still sinners, Christ died for us." As mentioned above, this is not merely mental assent but a conscious decision to trust Christ personally.

Much like a wedding-day commitment, it is a moment of conscious decision to follow Christ (though imperfectly) and cultivate a lifelong relationship—trusting that he is exactly who he said he is as recorded in Scripture.

CONFESS

Confess Jesus as your Lord. This doesn't mean you will never mess up again. Rather, it means you will serve him and learn his ways as you grow spiritually and as you continue to walk with him in fellowship. Romans 10:9: "If you confess with your mouth the Lord Jesus and believe in your heart that God has raised Him from the dead, you will be saved" (NKJV).

Here's a simple prayer you can pray. These words aren't magic. Again, this is not a formula. But if these words accurately reflect the motives of your heart, according to the truths of the Bible, you will become a Christian. You will have placed your faith in Christ and will have had your sins forgiven. You will look forward to an eternity with Jesus in heaven, and you will avoid the terrible time of tribulation that will soon come to the world. You will avoid eternity apart from God in what the Bible describes as the lake of fire. If you are ready to accept Jesus as your Savior, please pray this prayer now.

> Lord Jesus, I admit that I am a sinner. I have sinned against you, and sin separates me from you. I thank you that you died on the cross for me. You took my sins upon you and paid my penalty at the cross. I believe you are who you say you are—God in the flesh. I believe you died for my sins, and I believe you rose again. I want to accept your gift of salvation and, at this moment, I ask you to be my Savior. I thank you for this great forgiveness. I now have new life. I now claim you as my Savior and my Lord. In Jesus' name. Amen.

If you just prayed that prayer, you are a new creation. The Bible tells us that heaven is celebrating right now because of your decision (Luke 15:10). The Holy Spirit now indwells you and will guide you and keep you. You won't be perfect, but you are forgiven, and he will never leave you. His work in you has just begun. You are an adopted co-heir with Christ. You will one day live and reign with him in the millennial kingdom and forever in eternity.

Just a couple verses after the famous words in John 3:16, it says plainly, "Whoever believes in him is not condemned, but whoever does not believe stands condemned already because they have not believed in the name of God's one and only Son" (verse 18).

Furthermore, Paul says in Romans 8:1 that "there is now no condemnation for those who are in Christ Jesus." No condemnation. No wrath. No judgment. Your account is free and clear of any penalty. If you are truly a believer in Christ, all of your sins—past, present, and future—were paid for at the cross. Does that mean we can now sin with impunity? No, it means we commit to follow Christ, repent and confess when we fail, understand our sins are taken care of, and move forward in growing to become more like Christ out of a heart of gratitude for what he has done.

If you were on death row and someone offered to switch places with you, thankfulness would shape the desires of your heart and drive you to live worthy of the sacrifice that was made on your behalf. What that means for believers in concrete terms is that though we are far from perfect, we are ever aware of the cost of our salvation and want to live up to God's expectations.

This makes me think of a scene from the movie *Saving Private Ryan*. This film of historical fiction chronicles the first days of Operation Overlord (D-Day), the allied invasion of Normandy, France, that would turn the tide on the western front during World War II in Europe. The filmmakers depict war as it happened, in its brutal and gory detail, to reflect to the audience the dire odds and high costs of the army unit's mission. If you have seen it, you may recall the scene at the end of the movie (*spoiler alert*) when James Francis Ryan (played by actor Matt Damon), as an elderly man, visits the grave of Captain John H. Miller. Captain Miller (played by Tom Hanks) led a rescue team to reach Private Ryan, and Miller gave his life (along with a few other men) to complete this mission. In the moving scene, as Ryan stands before Miller's grave in Normandy, contemplating the sacrifice that was made in order to bring him home, he hopes, from Captain Miller's point of view, that the life Ryan went on to live merited the loss.

Then Ryan's wife walks over to join him, and he asks her if he has led a good life. She is surprised and somewhat confused. His wife looks at Miller's grave, and then back at Ryan. The gravity of the moment registers and she understands that Ryan is feeling the full weight of the sacrifice that was made on behalf of him, to be alive all these years later. Ryan's wife looks him in the eyes and reassures him that he has.

That should be the attitude we embody as we live out our salvation. When we take time to contemplate how holy God is, how sinful we are, and the incredible price that was paid for us to enter heaven, we can't help but to live a life of extreme gratitude and dedication. This should drive our thoughts, motives, actions, and attitudes. It doesn't mean we won't struggle with our fallen sinful nature—what Scripture calls our flesh—but it does mean that we should be growing to be more like Christ as we move through this life in anticipation of the next.

One day, all of this will come into sharp focus, when it is our time to stand before the Lord. Similar to the affirmation Ryan received from his wife, we long to hear the words from our Savior, "Well done, good and faithful servant! You have been faithful with a few things; I will put you in charge of many things. Come and share your master's happiness!" (Matthew 25:23).

CHAPTER 11

Can You Know for Sure?

Very truly I tell you, the one who believes has eternal life.

JOHN 6:47

Recently, my wife was watching one of those murder mystery shows where each documentary-style episode covers a specific case where the hard work of investigators was needed to put a murderer behind bars. Two things stood out to me. First was a comment that the investigator made about the brevity of life, how fragile it is, and how much we tend to take it for granted.

This is a healthy (though at first listen, seemingly morbid) fact to keep in mind. In truth, it is a perspective that is biblical. In Psalm 39, David wrote a song that captures the thought well. Part of the psalm goes, "Show me, LORD, my life's end and the number of my days; let me know how fleeting my life is" (verse 4).

DAVID

When the clock is ticking, we tend to sense a certain amount of healthy urgency. Creative projects (like writing this book) are accomplished only because there is a concrete deadline. That looming due date places a focus to the task that becomes motivation to get to work and make that work count. The same is true with our lives. When we recognize that time is ever moving forward and our days are limited, we are pressed to take stock of what matters and make the most of how best to use our time.

The second thing that stood out to me from the show was something said by the surviving mother of a young woman who was murdered. As the show was winding down and she shared her final thoughts, in tears, the mother said she hopes there is an afterlife.

The world needs to hear the good news that there is indeed an afterlife. Better yet, the world needs to hear the good news that people can know right now whether they are destined to go to heaven! The plain teaching of Scripture—as highlighted in the previous chapter—is that believers in Christ can know that they are going to heaven. That is what Christ secured for us at the cross.

I don't pretend to understand all the mystery that surrounds how redemption works, but I do know this: Christ died to secure our salvation and it is available to anyone who would call upon him for salvation. We cannot work for it. We cannot earn it. All we can do is fall on the mercy of God and ask him to save us.

We can believe in what we do not see because of the things that we have already seen. Let me explain. As I have already shared, through a careful study of Scripture, we can see that God has already fulfilled hundreds of specific prophecies. This is a built-in proof of authenticity. His track record is perfect. God is a promise keeper who has never broken a promise. And he has guaranteed that if we place our trust in Christ, we can be made right with God and go to heaven when we die or are raptured.

Already, Not Yet

As I write this chapter, my youngest son is gearing up for his freshman year in college. He has already been accepted. His name and credentials are all in the system. Tomorrow we're going to orientation, and he will register for his fall semester classes. So he is as good as there. But he has not moved into his dorm, stepped foot into a single class, met any of his professors, or eaten his first meal on campus. He is as good as there—positionally. But he is not yet there—literally.

For those of us who know Christ, we are in a similar scenario. Positionally, we are as good as there. But literally and physically speaking, our experiential heavenly citizenship will become a reality sometime in the future. One day—either by death or by rapture—we will enter heaven and see our Lord face to face.

As a follow-up to the previous chapter, I want to highlight an important truth that many who have heard the gospel for the first time often need to hear. Here is the truth: You can know for sure right now that you will be going to heaven in the future!

The most famous of all Bible verses, John 3:16, reads, "For God so loved the world that he gave his one and only Son, that whoever believes in him shall not perish but have eternal life."

If you have (i.e., currently possess) eternal life, by nature it does not end. In other words, eternal life starts now! In 1 John 5:12, we see this truth stated another way: "Whoever has the Son has life; whoever does not have the Son of God does not have life."

Also, eternal life tends to be regarded as the life we will enter in the future, after our death. But the phrase, as Jesus used it, was about bringing the life of this future into the present. Judaism taught that eternal life would appear only on God's last day, or in the age to come. John tells the Jesus story in a way that shows that this eschatological day of salvation has already arrived in the person of Jesus. Eternity has broken into history (John 1:1-14).

Often when I speak at conferences, I'll drive home the point that we as believers live from the future. What I mean by that is, while we celebrate the key events of the past—namely the death, burial, and resurrection of Christ—we look forward to his future return, when he will come and set everything right.

In Christianity we know what the future holds, and it is amazing. However, when the church avoids talking about eschatology, we miss the single most compelling reason to keep moving forward when times get tough—the fact that we will be in heaven with God for eternity, where there will be no brokenness, pain, separation, death, sin, or evil!

Eternal life starts in the present for the believer. The Holy Spirit is the down payment who displays that everything the Lord promises for the future will come to pass. It is as good as done. We're simply not there on the timeline as of yet. Our quality of spiritual life today is driven and empowered by God's promises of never-ending life for our future.

What Difference Does It Make?

Understanding that we cannot work for salvation in the first place should set our minds at ease knowing we cannot lose it. It is eternal by nature. It was purchased by the blood of Christ. We did not contribute a single thing to earn it. Mankind is not just sin *sick*. We are completely spiritually *dead*. When we come to know Christ, we move from death to life. In other words, we did not earn salvation by our merits or power, and we cannot lose it by our failures. If that were the case, we would be losing our salvation daily.

But it's not possible for us to lose our salvation. Here are some Scripture passages that assure us of the security of our salvation:

> All those the Father gives me will come to me, and whoever comes to me I will never drive away. For I have come down from heaven not to do my will but to do the will of him who sent me. And this is the will of him who sent me, that I shall lose none of all those he has given me, but raise them up at the last day. For my Father's will is that everyone who looks to the Son and believes in him shall have eternal life, and I will raise them up at the last day (John 6:37-40).

> My sheep listen to my voice; I know them, and they follow me. I give them eternal life, and they shall never perish; no one will snatch them out of my hand. My Father, who has given them to

me, is greater than all; no one can snatch them out of my Father's hand (John 10:27-29).

You also were included in Christ when you heard the message of truth, the gospel of your salvation. When you believed, you were marked in him with a seal, the promised Holy Spirit, who is a deposit guaranteeing our inheritance until the redemption of those who are God's possession—to the praise of his glory (Ephesians 1:13-14).

When we live this life from the mindset and position of knowing that our salvation is secure, it allows us to move forward with confidence on our journey toward heaven. We grow to be more like Christ out of a spirit of thankfulness for what he has already done, not in an effort to gain his approval. For the believer, that matter is settled. Paul tells us in Romans 8:1, "There is *now no condemnation* for those who are in Christ Jesus."

Really coming to grips with this truth helps us look forward to our guaranteed future with Jesus in heaven. We can wonder what our custom living spaces in the Father's house will be like. We can contemplate what it will be like to have glorified bodies fit for heaven. We can ponder what it will be like to meet Moses, Adam, Abraham, Mary, Job, Isaiah, Daniel, Joseph, Ruth, or Queen Esther. We can consider what it will be like to stand before our Lord and see his nail-scarred hands with our own glorified eyes.

Job lived during the time period of the great Old Testament patriarchs before the law of Moses. Yet even back then he was able to say, "I know that my redeemer lives, and that in the end he will stand on the earth. And after my skin has been destroyed, yet in my flesh I will see God; I myself will see him with my own eyes—I, and not another. How my heart yearns within me!" (Job 19:25-27).

That should be our response. Our hearts should be near bursting from our chests as we use our God-given imagination to entertain thoughts about our promised future and all that it entails. We will see our Redeemer-God, and only then will it all make sense. As Paul puts it, "Now we see only a reflection as in a mirror; then we shall see face to face. Now I know in part; then I shall know fully, even as I am fully known" (1 Corinthians 13:12).

And John gives this perspective: "Dear friends, now we are children of God, and what we will be has not yet been made known. But we know that when Christ appears, we shall be like him, for we shall see him as he is" (1 John 3:2). At the rapture, you and I who name the name of Christ will come to know fully, and we will have resurrected, glorified bodies like the body of Jesus. We will be completely transformed in mind and body. We can be confident all this is true; we can know this for sure!

CHAPTER 12

What Does the Bible Say About Hell?

He will say to those on his left, "Depart from me, you who are cursed, into the eternal fire prepared for the devil and his angels."

MATTHEW 25:41

My wife was a teacher for many years before working as a curriculum specialist for the county in which we live. One year, the middle school where she worked was undergoing some construction, adding more classrooms to the building. During this time there were brief periods when there were several small openings at the end of the unfinished hallways. Couple this detail with the fact that the school backed up to a heavily wooded area inhabited by a wide variety of wildlife—and you can probably guess what happened as a result.

In addition to the extraordinary organisms known as middle school students that made their way into the school by day, other creatures of various types would find their way into the school by night. Various furry or scaled critters from the nearby habitat would follow their curious instincts, which led them right into the school.

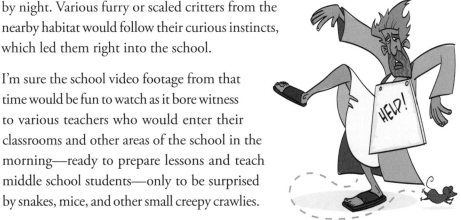

I'm sure the school video footage from that time would be fun to watch as it bore witness to various teachers who would enter their classrooms and other areas of the school in the morning—ready to prepare lessons and teach middle school students—only to be surprised by snakes, mice, and other small creepy crawlies.

The critters that wreaked the most havoc were the mice. Not only did they find their way into the school, they set up shop in the ceilings and walls, where they rapidly multiplied. Each morning would provide ample evidence of their nocturnal activity as various snacks and treats meant for students or stashed away in teachers' drawers were routinely found broken into as the mice foraged through their newfound environment full of caches of food.

Wherever the furry four-footed thieves pilfered various food products, they would leave small pieces of evidence that showed the food had been eaten and digested. Yuck! The new and ready-made living environment was adored by the mice, but it created obvious problems for the teachers, staff, and students at the school.

As the mice population quickly exploded, the maintenance team had no choice but to set out scores of mousetraps in the teachers' rooms, bathrooms, break rooms, and storage areas. Each morning as the teachers entered their rooms, they would wrestle with their competing emotions of hopeful anticipation and fearful reservation. On one hand, they wanted the mice to be caught. On the other hand, they cringed at the thought of peeking into the traps because of what they might find. There are some places that we just do not want to look in fear of what we may find.

We tend to approach the doctrine of hell in much the same way. We know that hell is necessary for the unrepentant Hitlers, Mussolinis, Genghis Khans, child abusers, and human traffickers of the world. But at the same time, we are a bit timid to look into the doctrine too deeply for fear of what we may find. We hear the postmodern complaints of a seemingly capricious and angry God who judges and pours out his wrath, and we wrestle with the details of the doctrine.

Why Include Hell in a Book About Heaven?

I can't write a book about heaven without also addressing the doctrine of hell. Heaven is that much more meaningful because of the reality of hell. We are eternal creatures, and we get to choose our destination. There are certain doctrines in Scripture that are difficult for us to accept. One of those is often the doctrine of hell. Much of this is because we truly don't realize the horrific effects of sin. We have never seen creation unmarred by its ugliness. We've never lived in a sinless state, so we can't even fully appreciate our own sinfulness.

The famous author C.S. Lewis wrote:

> There is no doctrine which I would more willingly remove from Christianity than this, if it lay in my power. But it has the full support of Scripture and, specially, of Our Lord's own words; it has always been held by Christendom; and it has the support of reason. If a game is played, it must be possible to lose it.[12]

The bottom line is Scripture tells us unequivocally that hell is real, it is necessary, and Jesus talked more about hell than he did heaven and many other topics (see Matthew 5:22; 8:8-12; 18:9; 23:33; 25:41; Mark 9:43). In fact, Jesus talked more about hell than any other person in the Bible. Why? Because Jesus doesn't want anyone to go there. To go to hell, people have to harden their hearts, ignore the truth of creation, and jump over the cross. In one sense, hell is answered prayer. People spend a lifetime rejecting Christ, demanding to be apart from him. Hell is the answer to this request, as it is the complete absence of his presence.

C.S. LEWIS

When we perform a careful survey of the Gospels, we find that Jesus himself described hell as a literal place, and our Savior provided a lot of details. Jesus described it as a place of everlasting pain (Luke 16:23), a place of unquenchable fire (Mark 9:43), a place of eternal worms (Mark 9:48), a place of immense regret where people will gnash their teeth in anguish (Matthew 13:42), a place of outer darkness (Matthew 25:30), and as a place from which there is no return and no second chance (Luke 16:19-31).

One of the most compelling comparisons Jesus used for the people of his day was that hell is a lot like Gehenna (Matthew 10:28). Gehenna was the city dump for Jerusalem. Not only was rotting trash perpetually burned there, but so were the carcasses of dead animals, and even dead criminals. It was a place of never-ending fire and stench. People stayed as far away from it as they could. That is the point our Lord was driving home with this comparison. He wants people to stay as far away from hell as possible. That was the whole reason for the cross.

FALLEN ANGELS · ANGELS

In fact, hell was originally created for the devil and the fallen angels (one-third of all the angels [Revelation 12:4]) who rebelled with him (Matthew 25:41). Once the fall of Adam and Eve took place in the garden, spiritual death entered the scene. Hell is the necessary and unavoidable just punishment for sin (Matthew 5:22). It is like a spiritual law of physics. It is simply a reality we do not fully grasp, but a reality nonetheless.

Hell as a Scare Tactic

I've heard people say statements similar to the following, "Hell is just a scare tactic." Is it? Or is it a flashing warning sign? When people see a fenced in area with a sign that reads HIGH VOLTAGE! KEEP OUT! they don't respond to it as a scare tactic. They view it as a warning. It is a sign that is posted with the intention to keep them safe. The same is true for the Bible's teachings about hell. Hell is a reality. Hell is horrible. Hell is necessary. Most importantly, hell is avoidable! That is why Jesus talked about it so frequently. Much of his ministry was dedicated to posting "Danger—Keep Out!" signs. Then Jesus personally went to the cross to make sure that we could!

But as with other teachings in the Bible, the enemy has done a great job of twisting the doctrine and lying about the reality of hell. People wonder why good people go to hell. Good people don't! None of us are good. None of us are righteous. That is the whole point. The real question is: Why would a holy God allow bad people into heaven? Because God so loved the world! God provided a way for sinful mankind to obtain righteousness when there was no way.

Levels of Punishment in Hell

Just as there are degrees of reward in heaven, there are degrees of punishment in hell. Luke 12:42-48 describes varying degrees of punishment symbolized by receiving either many or few lashes. To be blunt, Hitler will suffer far worse than the average lost soul in hell.

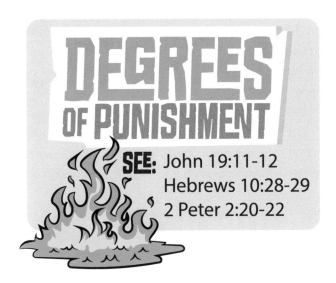

Carefully notice the last four words in Revelation 20:12-13:

> I saw the dead, the great and the small, standing before the throne, and books were opened; and another book was opened, which is the book of life; and the dead were judged from the things which were written in the books, according to their deeds (NASB).

According to their deeds. One thing we always need to keep in mind when considering eternal punishment is that God is 100 percent fair in his dealings. Someone has to pay for our sins because we can't get right with God on our own.

Jesus paid the penalty and offers us the most amazing gift ever given. It is free to us, but it cost him everything.

If we reject God's offer to pay our sin debt, then we are 100 percent fairly judged based on our specific actions while we lived. Unfortunately, if we want separation from Christ in this life, he has no choice but to answer that prayer in the afterlife. The truest definition of hell is complete separation from God.

In Revelation, John mentions that the lake of fire is the second death. Recall that in Scripture, we learn there are two births and two deaths. Natural birth occurs when we are physically born, and spiritual birth when we accept Christ (John 3:3-6). Natural death takes place when our physical bodies die, and there is a second spiritual death that John refers to as the lake of fire. So if you are born twice, you die once; but if you are born once, you die twice.

Progressive Revelation of the Afterlife

There are certain aspects about heaven and hell that people have overly simplified or dumbed down because of assumptions that there are many who can't handle the details. I believe that they can. I believe that when we dig into the weeds, the story rings true, the theology makes more sense, and believers gain a much better idea of the backstory, along with all of its implications for time and eternity.

Early biblical writers understood the key aspects of the afterlife. Over time, God revealed more information. In systematic theology, this is known as progressive revelation. The Old Testament understanding of the afterlife was summed up in the Hebrew word *Sheol*. This was a broad term which could mean the unseen realm of the dead (Genesis 37:35), the actual grave where someone was buried (Psalm 141:7), a place of punishment (Psalm 55:15; Isaiah 5:14; Hosea 13:14), or a holding area for the Old Testament-era righteous after they died (Psalms 49:15; 86:13). Context is key in determining which of these is being indicated by a passage.

In the New Testament, the Greek word for this holding place of the dead is *Hades*. Sheol, or Hades, is always depicted as being downward, under the earth's crust, under mountains, the lower regions of the earth, yet in the unseen realm. The parallel realities mysteriously coexist. Sheol generally has negative, punitive connotations—with the one exception that we highlighted in chapter 3 about paradise/Abraham's side, when we previewed some glimpses of heaven that are provided for us in Scripture.

Just to recap, Abraham was the father of promise. God's chosen people and the Savior of the world came from Abraham. The whole earth has indeed been blessed through Abraham's descendant (Genesis 22:18). Prior to the cross, all of the righteous dead went to this comforting and blessed holding place of promise. We read about this in Luke 16. In that chapter, Jesus shared an account that sheds tremendous light on the subject. And remember, it is important to recognize that this was not a parable but is described as an actual account.

ABRAHAM

If you will recall, Jesus told the one thief who believed in him while on the cross that the thief would be with him in paradise that day. We also learn in Ephesians 4:8-9 that Jesus moved the location of paradise to heaven between the time of his death and resurrection. I cover this at length in my book *The Non-Prophet's Guide™ to Spiritual Warfare*. We also find that in the future, the current hell—or place of torment spoken of in the story of the rich man and Lazarus—will be relocated into the lake of fire, where it will remain for all eternity.

The first two residents of the lake of fire will be the future antichrist and his false prophet. In Revelation 19:20, we read,

> The beast was captured, and with it the false prophet who had performed the signs on its behalf. With these signs he had deluded those who had received the mark of the beast and worshiped its image. The two of them were thrown alive into the fiery lake of burning sulfur.

Then in Revelation 20:14-15, we learn that the rest of the unsaved will join them there. In that passage we read,

> Then death and Hades were thrown into the lake of fire. The lake of fire is the second death. Anyone whose name was not found written in the book of life was thrown into the lake of fire.

The Bottom Line

We don't know where hell is located because it is in an unseen dimension, but it is often depicted as being downward and associated with the grave. Descriptions of hell let us know that it is otherworldly. It is seen as a place of fire, yet at the same time, a place of outer darkness. It is the complete absence of the experiential presence of God. It is—sadly—giving people what they want when they choose to reject Christ.

Hell will be a place of unending pain of various degrees based on the works of an individual. It will be eternal separation from all that is good and fulfilling. Worse yet, one day in the future it will be thrown into the lake of fire.

Like a prison within a prison, hell will be like an Alcatraz cast into the vast, permanent, and unescapable bay of God's just judgment.

Thankfully, hell is not the only option. God has made a way out. The word *gospel* means "good news." The good news of the gospel is that Jesus has reconciled us with the Father. He took our punishment so that we do not have to receive it. We need to share this news with a lost and dying world that desperately needs to hear it! The reality of hell makes the glory of heaven shine all the brighter, and makes it even more attractive.

One final thought before we move on to the next chapter: I think one reason we tend to cringe at the idea that hell is a literal place where people will exist is that we do not fully grasp the nature, depth, and ugliness of sin. We are like fish in an ocean that do not realize how wet they are, nor how deep the ocean is. We are so immersed in the fallenness of this world that we cannot truly see how bad our own sin is. Our fallen nature keeps us from seeing the true depth of two things: the holiness of God and the sinfulness of mankind.

But in the pure light of heaven when we have our sinless, glorified bodies, we will not question for a millisecond that there is an absolute need for hell, even though we cannot fully comprehend or appreciate it now. This is yet another doctrine that we must accept by faith.

SECTION 4:

SECONDARY QUESTIONS ABOUT HEAVEN

CHAPTER 13

Our Fellowship in Heaven

Now we see only a reflection as in a mirror; then we shall see face to face. Now I know in part; then I shall know fully, even as I am fully known.

1 CORINTHIANS 13:12

Sections 1–3 of this book have been establishing the biblical foundation for sections 4 and 5. They have been grounded in more of a chapter-and-verse theological presentation. I have attempted to share clear-cut theology taken directly from the plain language of Scripture. I'm not implying that my theology is above correction or that I have all the answers, but I have attempted to lay out what we can understand from the clear teaching of Scripture using a literal, grammatical, plenary approach to interpreting the Bible.

I'm sure my personal bias is infused in my theology to some degree, and as I've written this book, I've attempted to handle the Word of God as accurately as possible. I take this responsibility very seriously, although imperfectly. I am well aware that being a student of the Bible is a lifetime pursuit and the more I study, the more I realize I don't know. But at the same time, the more I study, the deeper I love God's Word, and the more I am in awe to a greater degree of its depth and cohesiveness. In short, I have ventured to cut Scripture straight and accurately deliver what it has to say about heaven's current intermediate state, future development, and final eternal state.

I say all of this to point out that the next three chapters are somewhat more speculative in nature in the sense that we don't have passages that provide direct answers on certain matters. For this reason, I cannot be as authoritative about what I will share in all the topics we will take on. That said, I have done my best to point out what I believe we can see clearly stated in Scripture, verses that lend themselves to allow for what I call *sanctified speculation*. What I mean by that somewhat tongue-in-cheek term is that I will attempt to answer some questions based on *principles* that we find in Scripture, rather than clear and specific verses that state a particular truth of the Bible.

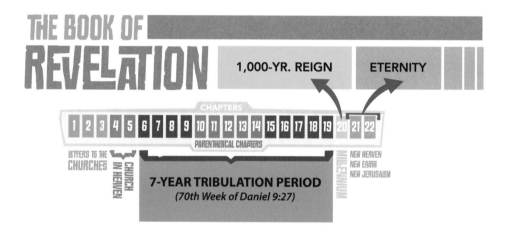

Seven Principles

It is important to note that in the book of Revelation we are given 14 chapters about the details concerning the final seven years of human history (Revelation 6–19), one chapter about the 1,000-year kingdom that follows it (Revelation 20), and two chapters about all of eternity (Revelation 21–22). We are not given the same amount of information about the specific details concerning each epoch of history. Therefore, it is important that we do not read more into Scripture than what it allows, even though I do believe we can deduce many details about heaven from some clear principles established within

Scripture. With that said, here are seven principles I will endeavor to apply when answering the questions that we pose in the following three chapters.

Principle #1: Where Scripture is silent, we must trust God and allow room for mystery.

The guiding verse for this principle is Deuteronomy 29:29, which reads, "The secret things belong to the LORD our God, but the things revealed belong to us and to our children forever, that we may follow all the words of this law." In other words, God has not revealed everything we may want to know, but what he has revealed is enough for us to know, follow, and trust him with our eternity (or any other biblical topic).

Principle #2: Whatever we imagine (or deduce from Scripture) about what heaven will be like, it pales in comparison to the reality of what we will experience once we are there.

First Corinthians 2:9 tells us, "No eye has seen, no ear has heard, and no mind has imagined what God has prepared for those who love him" (NLT). Jesus also tells us about God's unsurpassed generous character:

> Which of you, if your son asks for bread, will give him a stone? Or if he asks for a fish, will give him a snake? If you, then, though you are evil, know how to give good gifts to your children, how much more will your Father in heaven give good gifts to those who ask him!" (Matthew 7:9-11).

The God who created everything has a place in store for us that is beyond our comprehension and is—provided only in his power—very good.

Principle #3: We see a continuity of events and God's character in Scripture that should give us some insight into what the final eternal state will be like.

The foundational verses for this principle are James 1:17 and Hebrews 13:8. James wrote, "Every good and perfect gift is from above, coming down from the Father of the heavenly lights, who does not change like shifting shadows" (1:17). And in his closing remarks, the writer of Hebrews proclaims, "Jesus Christ is the same yesterday and today and forever" (13:8). When you view God's track record throughout the Bible, he has shown time and again that he is unchanging. Heaven will be what he's promised it to be, and it will reflect who we know God to be right now—God's character always remains the same.

Principle #4: Before the fall, mankind was created as image-bearers of God and called to extend his glory everywhere.

From the very beginning, God had purpose for human beings. This principle is seen in Genesis 1:27-28: "So God created mankind in his own image, in the image of God he created them; male and female he created them. God blessed them and said to them, 'Be fruitful and increase in number; fill the earth and subdue it.'" Humanity's purpose to give glory to God is unchanged.

Principle #5: Whatever was marred by sin and decay, God redeems, restores, and resurrects to an even better state than what was originally created.

The guiding verses for this principle are found in Romans 8:22-23:

We know that the whole creation has been groaning as in the pains of childbirth right up to the present time. Not only so, but we ourselves, who have the firstfruits of the Spirit, groan inwardly as we wait eagerly for our adoption to sonship, the redemption of our bodies.

Principle #6: God is our loving heavenly Father, and we are joint heirs with Christ, destined to share in his glory.

As God's children, believers are included in experiencing his glory. Verses that establish this principle are:

> 1 John 3:1—"See what great love the Father has lavished on us, that we should be called children of God! And that is what we are!"

> Romans 8:17—"If we are children, then we are heirs—heirs of God and co-heirs with Christ, if indeed we share in his sufferings in order that we may also share in his glory."

Principle #7: We should use a literal approach to interpreting Scripture.

As mentioned before, this does not mean Scripture does not use poetic or symbolic language. But where Scripture offers plain facts that would have been understood by the original audience as plain facts, we should be careful to take God's Word at face value.

With all that said, I'll do my best to answer some questions about our fellowship and relationships in heaven.

Will I Be Married in Heaven?

The short answer is no, but yes. This first question may surprise you as you may have been expecting a question related to our fellowship with Christ. Well, you were correct! This is actually two questions in one. Jesus is the Bridegroom, and the church is the bride of Christ. There is something about our union with Christ after the rapture that is so profound that our best, most idealistic ideas about marriage in this fallen world merely point to the ultimate reality of our union with Christ once we are in heaven.

Our intimate fellowship with Christ will be so complete, so fulfilling, so perfect that all of our needs for intimacy, oneness, and deep fellowship will be fully and finally realized beyond our imagination. Knowing our Savior on an entirely new level and seeing him face to face will be more compelling, gratifying, and rewarding than anything we have ever experienced on earth.

In light of this, there will be no need for human marriage as we know it. The first part of God's mandate to Adam and Eve, "be fruitful and multiply" (Genesis 1:28), will no longer be necessary because, in eternity, there will be no more new beings. In Luke 20:34-36, Jesus said,

> The people of this age marry and are given in marriage. But those who are considered worthy of taking part in the age to come and in the resurrection from the dead will neither marry nor be given in marriage, and they can no longer die; for they are like the angels. They are God's children, since they are children of the resurrection.

The Sadducees whom Jesus was responding to here were posing a hypothetical scenario about marriage in the age of the resurrection; however, they were positioning it from the context of the age in which they were in. Jesus provided an answer for them that not only reflected the truth about what will be, but also that draws attention to the perspective from which it is to be viewed, the context of the age to come. This is an important lesson for us.

In short, eternal, supernatural beings—which we will be in our eternal state—do not marry. We will not have (or need, or desire) sexual relations. I will be careful to be tactful here because I know that people of a wide range of ages read my books, but this is a question of great importance to some as they contemplate heaven and what it will be like.

So I'll just say that similarly to how children before puberty are not drawn to the gift of physical intimacy (which was intended solely for use in the context of a marriage between a man and a woman), our sense of intimacy in heaven will be so fulfilling and continually complete that we will not miss anything.

In fact, our best pleasures in this life are mere types that point to a greater reality in heaven. Shadows indicate only a hint of something much greater and considerably more substantive. If you'll recall principle 2 above, our greatest imagined bliss in this life will not hold a candle to how completely and permanently fulfilled and satisfied we will feel in heaven at every moment of our eternal existence.

We will crave nothing. We will lack no good thing. We will experience true intimacy unmarred by sin and unlike anything we have experienced or hope to experience in this life. As a caterpillar has no concept of flying, we have no real concept of how good heaven will be on every single level. We must trust God with how this will play out because we cannot truly conceive of its fulfillment.

I also want to mention that although we will not be married to our spouses in heaven (for those of us who are married), our relationship with them will be better than it has ever been. In fact, our fellowship with all believers—including loved ones who have gone before us, giants of the faith in the Bible and from church history, and even believers we had difficulty getting along with in this life—will be perfect in every way.

Will Children (Including the Unborn) Be in Heaven?

This question comes up often when I discuss the doctrine of the rapture. People want to know what happens to the preborn, infants, toddlers, and young children who die or will be raptured before they understand their need to accept Christ as their Savior. Principle 1 applies here. There are not specific verses that make definitive statements on the matter; therefore, we must trust God with the results. That said, we can also take what we know about God's character (principle 3) and look at a few verses that can give some insight into the matter.

In 2 Samuel 12:22-23, after King David's first child with Bathsheba died, David stated,

> While the child was still alive, I fasted and wept. I thought, "Who knows? The LORD may be gracious to me and let the child live." But now that he is dead, why should I go on fasting? Can I bring him back again? I will go to him, but he will not return to me.

These words show us David, a man after God's own heart, believed that someday he will reside in the same place as his child, who died when he was only seven days old.

The Bible also shows us Jesus' attitude toward children in Matthew 19:13-14, where we read,

> People brought little children to Jesus for him to place his hands on them and pray for them. But the disciples rebuked them. Jesus said, "Let the little children come to me, and do not hinder them, for the kingdom of heaven belongs to such as these."

Those two verses give us insight into God's love of children and how it likely relates to eternity. It also implies that people are responsible for what they are capable of understanding. I personally believe there is an age of accountability of sorts (which is probably different for each person) when a person is mentally and emotionally capable enough to know right from wrong. We are to respond to whatever light is given to us. The greater our knowledge and understanding, the greater our responsibility to respond. Scripture even implies that those who do not know God's expectations and naturally do things deserving of punishment will experience a lesser punishment in eternity (Luke 12:48). Just as there are degrees of reward in heaven, it seems there will be degrees of punishment in hell. Throughout Scripture there is an inherent tension between human responsibility and God's sovereignty. We must live with that tension by faith.

Will Pets or Animals Be in Heaven?

As I travel and speak, this question often comes up as well. People love their pets and want to see them in heaven. When it comes specifically to pets, I must appeal to principle 1. Scripture does not make a definitive statement. Both animals and humans have "the breath of life," but only humans were created in the image of God.

Though God may have some surprise gifts for us in heaven, possibly even a reunion with our family pets. Paul says:

> The creation itself will be liberated from its bondage to decay and brought into the freedom and glory of the children of God. We know that the *whole* creation has been groaning as in the pains of childbirth right up to the present time (Romans 8:21-23).

So even the animal kingdom aches for restoration to its intended order. And we can be confident that the Lord will renew creation (principle 5). We discover examples of this restoration in the future millennial kingdom, where animals will no longer eat other animals (Isaiah 11:6-7; 65:25), and where venom will no longer be something to fear (Isaiah 11:8). The future kingdom age serves as an overture to the eternal state—a foretaste of all that is to come. Therefore, I think it is very likely that animals will be in heaven for eternity.

In any case, one thing we know we can count on is we will not feel any sadness, longing, nor heartache about our pets if they are not present in heaven (Isaiah 65:17). Again, we can't imagine what our existence will be like (principle 2). Heaven will be lived on another plane of existence, but Scripture supplies many clues about what it will be like.

It does appear that animals or heavenly creatures with animal-like features will be in heaven. In Revelation 19:11-14, we read about Jesus returning to earth on a white horse followed by the armies of heaven, also on white horses. We looked at this event in detail in chapter 7. The armies are the angelic armies and the church. And recall our discussion from chapter 3, when we saw glimpses of God's throne room that are present in the Bible. We saw that there are other heavenly beings that have features like those of animals, such as the four living creatures that are around the throne of God who resembled a lion, an ox, a man, and an eagle. With all of the variety that God created in Genesis 1, there is no reason to believe there will be any less creativity and variety in the future eternal state.

Vertical, Horizontal, and Internal

The fellowship we will experience in heaven will be like nothing we have experienced before. Our vertical relationship—our fellowship with God—will be perfect. We will fellowship with him face to face. We will no longer have a sin nature. Our horizontal relationships—those with other believers from all ages—will likewise be perfect. But there is another aspect of our existence in heaven that we need to consider: our personal identity, which includes our calling, assignments, and eternal purpose. Who we will be in eternity is what we will discuss in the next chapter.

CHAPTER 14

Our Identity in Heaven

They triumphed over him by the blood of the Lamb and by the word of their testimony.

REVELATION 12:11

One of the things I find interesting about the present time in church history is that the enemy has been able to convince large numbers in the church (particularly in the West) that the book of Genesis is not to be interpreted literally. They believe it is mere allegory, and that when it comes to the account of creation, we really don't know how God worked, how long ago it occurred, or how long it took to complete.

Without a doubt, this is a result of the thinking of the modern era, where liberal theology has undermined the authority of the Bible and convinced millions that the Bible is merely a book about mankind's attempt to live a moral life and that Jesus was merely a good person—a model to follow.

DAYS OF CREATION

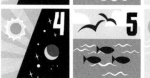

ON DAY 7 GOD RESTED/FINISHED CREATION

During the same timeframe, the theory of evolution and the powerful march of naturalism took root at every level in colleges, universities, and government agencies. In short, the belief in a literal six-day creation is not in vogue, and this has led many in the church to neglect teaching it. Worse yet, many church leaders no longer believe it.

The reason this is so heartbreaking is that Genesis provides the foundation for everything related to the gospel itself. If Genesis 1–3 do not provide us with an accurate history on how God created all things, how sin entered into the world, how death was introduced, and how God was going to fix it, then how can we know whether we can trust the rest of the Bible? This is the reason there are many who say the Bible is built on fables. I don't know about you, but I can't put my trust in something that is alleged to be fables. I must follow truth.

I bring this up for a reason. Everyone wants to know their origins. Children always want to know where they came from and about the events that surrounded their birth. The popularity of genealogy research has seen a significant boom in recent years. It is hardwired into us to want to understand two things: where we came from and where we are going.

There is something about our origins that feeds into our personhood—our very identity. It is what lies at the heart of many false and sure-to-fail movements in our day. People want to identify as something else. In reality they crave salvation and life change, but they are looking for love in all the wrong places. Christ alone can change us, and this truth is founded in the account of our origins.

In the context of this book, this raises a key question. What will our identity be in heaven? In other words, will we have our same personality, sense of humor, interests, talents, and knowledge base? I believe the answer is yes but with one key qualifier. We will be everything we are now, but in glorified form without any sin nature or sin-cursed limitations.

Cartography and Bible Prophecy

It is very interesting to look back through history and view the work of cartographers from the time before manned flight. They would use various means and tools to take measurements on land as they traveled on foot or by horseback. They cruised waterways and sailed around coastlines, calculating distances and making observations. There are many comical misconceptions of what the continents look like from some early mediocre cartography work.

Imagine someone painting the Mona Lisa from memory or from hearing detailed descriptions. It could resemble the real thing, but likely will miss some details and have very wrong proportions.

But there were also some very careful and meticulous cartographers who produced some surprisingly accurate maps without the aid of aircraft or satellites. Several of these maps are very recognizable (yet imperfect) when compared with the modern images we are capturing from space. Though some proportions and distances depicted in these early maps were off, basic shapes are recognizable, and overall, they were accurate when it came to representing all the main features of what the cartographers set out to represent.

I see this historical development of cartography as an analogy for Bible prophecy. Like large mountains or bays in relation to mapmaking, some of the prominent features of Bible prophecy and eschatology are fairly easy to reference and identify. But smaller or more obscure details, the connections with the prominent features and any unknown regions, are tougher to map out. Abiding in God's Word with great care will bring us greater clarity. We will be able to cast our vision closer to the reality that we will experience in the future kingdom age and eternal state.

Currently in our understanding, we hug the coastlines provided by Scripture to paint a picture of our future, but one day we will live in the very existence we are striving to chart and the level of detail will be like divine satellite imagery. Our job here in the present is to do our best to paint a faithful and accurate picture to the best of our ability so we can communicate to others what we are hopeful for in the future.

Continuity Further Explained

From the previous chapter, principle 3 highlights the fact that we see a continuity of events and God's character in Scripture that should give us some insight into what the final eternal state will be like.

In addition to James 1:17 and Hebrews 13:8, I will also appeal to the clear teaching in Scripture that there are successive eras of biblical history (dispensations) to highlight God's consistency in action and in character. Back in chapter 8, we discussed how the framework of dispensations helps to tell the narrative of the story of the Bible. Some of the following will be review, but here I will discuss dispensations again, only this time with the goal of showing how dispensations relate to one another.

Paul speaks about the dispensation of the church age, and he referred to it as "the dispensation of the grace of God" (Ephesians 3:2 NKJV). Other translations call it "the administration of God's grace" (NIV) or "the stewardship of God's grace" (ESV). The word translated "dispensation," "administration," or "stewardship" is the Greek word *oikonomia*. It is the same word Jesus used in the parable of the shrewd manager, found in Luke 16:1-15, where, for a time, a man was given the responsibility of managing a rich person's possessions.

In the United States, when there is a transition from the current president to a new president, we commonly say we are under a new administration. Each new administration does things differently than the administration before it,

but each continues to build with previous events and conditions in consideration. The fundamental structure remains the same, but how the new administration operates changes in certain ways, though not in all.

I believe the clear teaching of Scripture is that there have been different eras, periods, "dispensations," "economies," "administrations," or *oikonomia* through which the Lord has operated. The broad term for this point of view is dispensationalism, which highlights these different eras in Bible interpretation.

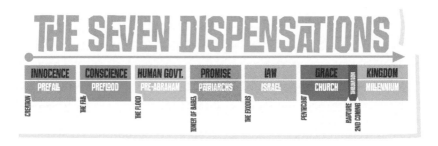

Salvation always comes to mankind by grace through faith, looking forward or backward to the Redeemer, and is based on what people knew in their particular time period. Broadly speaking, the Bible communicates one story of creation, fall, redemption, and restoration. But this story has also played out through the different *oikonomia*.

All of that to say, in each era there is a carryover from the previous eras. Each period, with the exception of the first, does not start from scratch but carries with it various conditions from the previous eras. The dispensations relate to one another and build off each other, each one having hints of the eras that have come before. As we saw previously, even if we skip stages by jumping from Genesis 1–2 to Revelation 21–22, we find that there is a continuity in God's work of redemption and restoration.

CONTINUITY

So in regard to the millennial kingdom and the eternal state, I believe we would expect to see a continuity present, a building upon previous redemptive history with evil and sin being purged out progressively. During the kingdom age, church-age believers will be sinless with glorified bodies. However, tribulation-era saints will enter the 1,000-year reign of Christ with their sin nature and natural bodies intact.

Satan will be bound during that time, but he will be released at the end of it. He will attempt one last temptation of the descendants of those who survived the tribulation period. Finally, in the eternal state, all evil will have been judged, sin will have been completely purged from creation, heaven and earth will be restored as one, and these conditions will be set in stone for eternity.

All of this continuity informs how we think about the future eternal state and what it will be like. It helps inform us about the answers we have relating to our identity in the questions below. That said, I want to restate that I can't be dogmatic or authoritative in answering the following questions. They are an attempt to apply what we do know to things we don't know.

How Old Will People Be in Heaven?

This is one of those questions for which we need to first apply Deuteronomy 29:29 (principle 1). We can't state with authority what age we will appear during eternity, but there are some clues found in Scripture that I believe can give us a possible indication.

If you recall, 1 John 3:2 states, "What we will be has not yet been made known. But we know that when Christ appears, we shall be like him, for we shall see him as he is." Again, we will receive glorified bodies fit for heaven at the moment of the rapture. Jesus began his ministry when he was around 30 years old and had this ministry for three-and-a-half years before the events of the cross and the resurrection. His disciples recognized him, so he must have looked the same (even though Jesus could also veil his identity) (Luke 24).

We also find that when God created Adam and Eve, they were fully developed adults. Similarly, when God created the trees, grass, land animals, fish, and birds, they were fully developed and in their mature state. Even the stars and galaxies—though millions of light-years away—were created with their light already reaching earth, the focal point of creation and the habitation of God's image bearers.

So it is my belief that the most likely scenario is that everyone in heaven will appear and function in their prime of life. The unborn will be fully mature adults. The elderly who have gone before us will have their wrinkles reversed. I have heard it said that, at the rapture, we'll experience a facelift followed by an uplift!

Will People Automatically Know Each Other in Heaven?

So if everyone will be in their prime, mature condition, even if they died in the womb, this leads to another logical question: Will we know who everyone is in heaven?

Many of the principles of sanctified speculation are at play here, but I believe Scripture gives us a hint. In Matthew 17:1-6, when Peter, James, and John witnessed Jesus in his glorified form and joined by Moses and Elijah, the three disciples knew immediately who was talking with Jesus. It seems that we will know people intuitively. Again, our fellowship and connection with other believers will be perfect.

MOSES

ELIJAH

While this does not necessarily mean we will automatically know who everyone is in heaven, it does seem to indicate we'll know who the major biblical figures are. Perhaps part of our eternal bliss will include meeting everyone in heaven and learning their stories—all for the purpose of further celebrating the worthiness of the Lord and the eternal results of our redemption.

Can you imagine meeting martyrs from different times and locations who sacrificed their lives for the gospel? We'll meet people from every era of history and every region of the globe. We'll get to meet the prophets, the patriarchs, the apostles, the disciples, and the list goes on. Imagine having a conversation with Moses, a cup of coffee (or whatever beverage will be in heaven) with Job, and a walk with Adam. What we can say for sure is that whatever our interactions with others will entail, how rich our relationships will be, and to what depth we will know one another are aspects of eternity that are beyond our current comprehension.

Will Earthly Life Prepare People for Heaven?

Appealing to the principle of continuity that we established at the beginning of this chapter, coupled with what we learned in chapter 5 about the reward believers will be given at the judgment seat of Christ, I believe what we do now matters for eternity.

When we consider a few other verses, we gain more intel on what may await us in the millennial kingdom and eternity. In Ephesians 2:10, Paul reminds us that "we are God's handiwork, created in Christ Jesus to do good works, which God prepared in advance for us to do." We are God's masterpieces. He wired us and has lined up the good works that we will do. There is no reason to believe this means works done only in this life.

Luke 12:7 tells us God knows the exact number of hairs on our head at any given time. Along these same lines, we discover in the Psalms that God takes great care in every detail of our making and what is set in our future. Read the following verses carefully and slowly and be encouraged:

> For you created my inmost being; you knit me together in my mother's womb. I praise you because I am fearfully and wonderfully

made; your works are wonderful, I know that full well. My frame was not hidden from you when I was made in the secret place, when I was woven together in the depths of the earth. Your eyes saw my unformed body; all the days ordained for me were written in your book before one of them came to be. How precious to me are your thoughts, God! How vast is the sum of them! Were I to count them, they would outnumber the grains of sand—when I awake, I am still with you (Psalm 139:13-18).

And in Luke 11:11-13, we get a snapshot of the fatherly love God has for us. There, Jesus says,

> Which of you fathers, if your son asks for a fish, will give him a snake instead? Or if he asks for an egg, will give him a scorpion? If you then, though you are evil, know how to give good gifts to your children, how much more will your Father in heaven give the Holy Spirit to those who ask him!

Taking into consideration God's high level of care and intentionality, I cannot see how God would not use everything we go through in this earthly life to prepare us for our roles in the millennial kingdom and beyond. He has given us each a personality, background, spiritual gifts, abilities, knowledge, skills, and godly passions that are specific to each of us, down to the microscopic detail. I do not think we would then become cookie-cutter citizens of the kingdom of heaven.

He has given us outstanding variety in our makeup, abilities, gifts, and skills. I do not think there are a small number of roles in the kingdom and the eternal state. God is a God of creativity, diversity, beauty, and intellect. If anything, the kingdom and eternity will consist of many more of these characteristics, not any fewer!

Will We Remember the Past?

Isaiah 65:17 reads, "See, I will create new heavens and a new earth. The former things will not be remembered, nor will they come to mind."

Some people have used this single verse to overstate what is being said. I've heard individuals say that we will no longer remember anything about the past and it will be as if we have always lived in the eternal state. This sounds more like the philosophies of one of the Eastern religions than it does Christianity.

What this verse in Isaiah is really saying is that a new order will come. The pains of the old fallen world will no longer plague us. A good cross reference for this verse is Revelation 21:4, which reads, "'He will wipe every tear from their eyes. There will be no more death' or mourning or crying or pain, for the old order of things has passed away."

Again, remember that God works through post-creation history with continuity. Each new era or dispensation builds upon the previous one. Isaiah 65:17 does not tell us that we will not remember anything from the past, but instead, it shows that the sting of sin, death, decay, and corruption will no longer be felt or experienced. In fact, Revelation 22:3 plainly states, "No longer will there be any curse."

There will be no post-traumatic stress syndrome of any kind. We will be completely free and clear of all emotional baggage, fear, depression, anxiety, and struggle. We won't dwell on the pain of the past, but we will remember our earthly lives and how the Lord God redeemed us! Our redemption story is directly related to our worship. Jesus alone is worthy, and we will celebrate that for eternity.

Uniquely You

Given all of what you just read, you can rest assured that in eternity you will be uniquely you and I will be uniquely me. Believers' core identity will be in Christ, but Scripture is also clear that part of their personal story is the fact that they overcome evil by the blood of the Lamb and by the word of their testimony (Revelation 12:11). If you are a believer in Christ along with me, what an incredible future we have in store.

Our stories are uniquely ours. God brings out the most in who we are. Revelation 2:17 even mentions God will give the victorious a white stone with a new name on it. It says that the new name will be understood only by the individual who receives it.

Perhaps that new name will give meaning to your past and direction for your future. God is a giver of gifts, a loving Father, and a promise keeper. From our discussion thus far, I can't help but to postulate that God is now preparing us for eternity in many more ways than we even realize. Is there a ministry you've dreamed about that you won't get to do in this life? Perhaps the Lord is preparing an opportunity for you along those same lines in the millennial kingdom and beyond! We'll find out.

CHAPTER 15

Our Activity in Heaven

The sovereignty, power and greatness of all the kingdoms under heaven will be handed over to the holy people of the Most High. His kingdom will be an everlasting kingdom, and all rulers will worship and obey him.

DANIEL 7:27

A few years ago, when my age had surpassed my body's ability to absorb snowboard tumbles on a favorite ski mountain in Pennsylvania, I took a hard fall on the last run of the morning and achieved what is known as a grade-three shoulder separation.

You and I have three sets of ligaments that connect our collarbones to our shoulder blades. When I fell, I successfully destroyed all three sets. As a result, the end of my collarbone was free floating under my skin like the end of a diving board covered by a beach towel.

After a few screws, a cadaver tendon, and a surgical medical cord were used to connect everything together again, I enjoyed a few months of physical therapy and endured a year's worth of healing before I could get back to my normal routine.

People enjoy activities such as snowboarding, skiing, skydiving, rock climbing, hiking, kayaking, and others that allow them to experience creation and to have some adventure. There is inherent risk in undertaking these activities, but the desire to get out into the elements is innate to the human experience.

We naturally want to engage with the enormous playground God built for mankind to enjoy. This desire is not a result of Adam and Eve's fall; however, the risks involved in participation—such as the danger of getting a grade-three shoulder separation—are.

Heaven won't be any less interesting, adventurous, or engaging than our current existence on planet Earth. Heaven will be the most exciting journey of your existence, and it will never end. Prior to the eternal state, the millennial kingdom will also offer the same excitement but with the added purpose of making Christ known to the masses of people who will be the descendants of those who were saved during the tribulation period and survived to its end.

The verse at the beginning of this chapter, Daniel 7:27, is speaking to us about the timeframe of Jesus' everlasting kingdom. The millennial kingdom will serve as the front porch to eternity. It will be the overture to the main production. It will be a microcosm of the final eternal reality. As I have already mentioned, there is a continuity to God's activity throughout history. Everything is building toward the final eternal state, which will be the ultimate culmination of all things.

We've already established what our relationships will be like in heaven—at least to the best of my ability based on details provided in Scripture. And we've established a continuity of eras. We've even looked at believers' rewards and the fact that they will rule and reign with Christ. *But eternity is a long time* (pun intended). What in the world will we be doing forever? This chapter answers some of those questions.

What Will We Do in Heaven?

We may not know every nuance of what we will be doing, but here are the basic things Scripture clearly tells us we will be doing. We will rest (Revelation 14:13) and we will work (Revelation 22:3). Wait a minute. Why will we need rest? And why will we need to work? Let me put it this way: We will rest in our work. We will rest in the sense that we will be completely fulfilled in our work assignments and with opportunities. We won't work for money; we will work for purpose—and we will find our rest in that.

As part of our work-rest we will judge the world and angels (1 Corinthians 6:2-3), we will rule (2 Timothy 2:12; Revelation 20:6), we will be priests (1 Peter 2:9; Revelation 20:6), and we will worship (Daniel 7:27). So it looks like we're going to be very busy in heaven. In our glorified bodies, we will not need sleep, and we will be able to travel at the speed of thought, so we'll be able to get a lot done.

What Kinds of Work Will We Do in Heaven?

The term *work* often carries negative connotations. But in Scripture, God is seen as working. In John 5:17, Jesus said, "My Father is always at his work to this very day, and I too am working." (See also John 5:19-20.) If God works, then it makes sense that his created beings work and will continue to work. The writer of Hebrews informs us that angels work (Hebrews 1:7, 14), and John tells us we are fellow servants with them (Revelation 22:9).

Toilsome work is a result of the fall. In Genesis 3:17-19, God said to Adam,

> Because you listened to your wife and ate fruit from the tree about which I commanded you, "You must not eat from it," cursed is the ground because of you; through painful toil you will eat food from it all the days of your life. It will produce thorns and thistles for you, and you will eat the plants of the field. By the sweat of your brow you will eat your food until you return to the ground, since from it you were taken; for dust you are and to dust you will return.

And just before God spoke to Adam, he spoke to Eve, and outlined the curse of pain that would be experienced in childbirth, also a result of the fall. While fulfilling their role in the work of populating the earth, women have painful labor under the shadow of sin.

In heaven, both of these conditions of the curse—along with every other consequence of the fall—will be removed. Women won't bear children in heaven (and I suspect it is possible that in the millennial kingdom childbearing could be less painful than it is now). And work will not be toilsome or difficult. It will be a fulfilling part of who we are and what we are called to do.

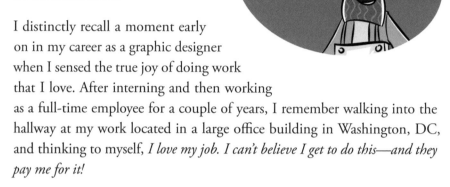

I distinctly recall a moment early on in my career as a graphic designer when I sensed the true joy of doing work that I love. After interning and then working as a full-time employee for a couple of years, I remember walking into the hallway at my work located in a large office building in Washington, DC, and thinking to myself, *I love my job. I can't believe I get to do this—and they pay me for it!*

Since then, I've felt that same impression several times in ministry. Don't get me wrong; work is still 1 percent inspiration and 99 percent perspiration—especially ministry work. But at this stage in my life and ministry, as I try to leverage everything the Lord has built into my past for his glory, there are moments when I need to pinch myself. I can't believe I get to do this.

I am well aware that not everyone loves their job or the line of work they are in. Maybe it is a hobby you have, a passion, a dream, or something else you've always wanted to do. When you think about it you feel free, invigorated, excited, and like you are in the zone. Now imagine that same sense of purpose multiplied by 1,000,000—with no toil, struggle, or mishaps. In heaven, there is no Murphy's Law—only God's law. In heaven, we will have purpose and a calling to the glory of God—forever!

Perhaps what we are doing now will be related to what we do in the future. Maybe we will pursue similar interests or things we've always wanted to do, only in a heavenly context. We'll have bodies fit for heaven and minds that understand our creator on a greater level than we do currently, but we will still be truly ourselves. It is not like we will start a new existence as a blank slate, minus a sin nature. Just as Jesus, Moses, and Elijah maintained their identity on the mount of transfiguration, we too will maintain our identities. We will be ourselves—but truly the best version of ourselves. Whatever we will be doing, it will fit us to a tee and be more rewarding and fulfilling than any work we've ever done in this life.

Will There Be Sports, Arts, Entertainment, and Technology in Heaven?

As it relates to this question, I believe the continuity principle and the fact that we will be the best version of ourselves gives us great insight into our future endeavors. Mankind was created in the image of God. Part of this means that we are creative, intelligent, story driven, and pursuers of true beauty in all its God-glorifying forms. This was made a part of us at creation. It was marred by the fall. And it will be restored and enhanced in the future.

Therefore, I believe there will most likely be sports, art, entertainment, and technology—or things that are even better. For example, sports involve creativity, story, enjoyment, and the thrill of accomplishment.

Many athletes, musicians, artists, and engineers clearly have God-given ability, and in the final eternal state, one can only imagine how much more these specialists (and everyone else) will be able to accomplish with glorified bodies and minds, with no sin nature, all to the glory of God!

As we've seen in Scripture, heaven will be a physical place with physical attributes, even though it will include supernatural aspects as well. Earlier in this book, we glimpsed at the physical nature of the new Jerusalem, but I think it is important to return to this subject in greater detail here by looking at some additional verses. Read the following depictions from the book of Revelation that describe the physical nature of the new Jerusalem.

First, we are introduced to the capital city, or headquarters, of heaven.

> I saw "a new heaven and a new earth," for the first heaven and the first earth had passed away, and there was no longer any sea. I saw the Holy City, the new Jerusalem, coming down out of heaven from God, prepared as a bride beautifully dressed for her husband (21:1-2).

Then we are provided with incredible details about the physical characteristics of the new Jerusalem.

> The angel who talked with me had a measuring rod of gold to measure the city, its gates and its walls. The city was laid out like a square, as long as it was wide. He measured the city with the rod and found it to be 12,000 stadia in length, and as wide and high as it is long. The angel measured the wall using human measurement, and it was 144 cubits thick. The wall was made of jasper, and the city of pure gold, as pure as glass. The foundations of the city walls were decorated with every kind of precious stone. The first foundation was jasper, the second sapphire, the third agate, the fourth emerald, the fifth onyx, the sixth ruby, the seventh chrysolite, the eighth beryl, the ninth topaz, the tenth turquoise, the eleventh jacinth, and the twelfth amethyst. The twelve gates were twelve pearls, each gate made of a single pearl. The great street of the city was of gold, as pure as transparent glass (verses 15-21).

What you just read is not allegory or symbolism. That is a clear description of the capital city of heaven, provided for us in the final book of the canon. By the way, the 12 precious stones mentioned in verses 19-20 are all anisotropic stones. That is a fancy scientific word that means in pure light, they display all the colors of the rainbow. There are many other precious stones, including diamonds, rubies, and garnets, but they are isotropic jewels. That is another fancy scientific word that means they lose all color when in pure light. And here's the kicker: This fact wasn't discovered until our generation. Yet 2,000 years ago, John recorded what was shown him, and all 12 of the foundational stones present in the new Jerusalem are anisotropic.

With that in mind, I want you to read one more verse from Revelation 21. In verse 23, we read, "The city does not need the sun or the moon to shine on it, for the glory of God gives it light, and the Lamb is its lamp."

So we learn from John's description that the pure light of God's glory will shine through the city and these 12 beautiful anisotropic precious stones. We can't even fully imagine the colors, the beauty, the purity, and the awesomeness of heaven. God's glory will be refracted throughout the city in a manner we cannot even comprehend. And that's only the capital city, not bringing to mention the vastness of the rest of the new heavens and the new earth!

The original call for Adam and Eve to subdue the earth and extend God's glory everywhere will remain our mandate in heaven. We will use our passions, assignments, abilities, talents, creativity, and rewards to do meaningful work that sets our souls on fire and glorifies God. All in a place that will be filled by God's glory and absent of the curse brought by sin. What could be better?

Connecting the Dots

Perhaps it is the artist in me, but when I was young, one of my favorite activities was connect the dots. I loved trying to guess what the picture was going to depict. Usually, there were surrounding elements that gave me hints about what it was. Often, it involved a character I was familiar with, so that provided further clues as to what the picture might show when I finished the art puzzle.

Thankfully the dots were numbered, so if I followed them carefully, paying attention to keep the numbers in the correct order, slowly but surely an accurate picture would emerge. Well, Scripture has given us dots to connect. It takes a bit of work to connect them, and we need to take care to avoid getting anything out of order or skipping any dots. But as we continue the faithful work of studying the details and the logic of Scripture, a beautiful picture of heaven begins to emerge.

Much like a connect-the-dots picture, our efforts will produce lines that may be a bit wiggly and imperfect. Yet at its core, the result resembles a true likeness to what God has revealed to us and what he has in store. This is what I have attempted to achieve in the past three chapters. Some of it has been sanctified speculation, but none of it (in my humble and studied opinion) is wild speculation.

We can only operate from the reference point that we have. Just as John did his best to describe what he saw in the book of Revelation, I've done my best to unpack what we can learn from Scripture about our fellowship, identity, and activity in heaven. But we must recognize that we discover details about heaven from the viewpoint of our fallen natural bodies, and only through the grace of the Holy Spirit. When considering the wonders of our fellowship, identity, and activity in heaven, we need to keep within the boundaries established by Scripture and use our seven principles as a guide. Remember principle 2: Whatever we imagine (or deduce from Scripture) about what heaven will be like, it pales in comparison to the reality of what we will experience once we are there. One day, we will have glorified spiritual bodies and we will see that our best earthly explanations in no way capture the beauty and grandeur of heaven.

Perhaps there will be colors we've never seen. Perhaps we'll be able to see sounds, hear smells, and taste colors. Heaven will truly be another plane of existence with continuity and connection to the past, but without any remnants from the fall. God will restore everything!

SECTION 5:

WHAT DIFFERENCE DOES HEAVEN MAKE NOW?

CHAPTER 16

Our Focus in Light of Heaven

Be very careful, then, how you live—not as unwise but as wise, making the most of every opportunity, because the days are evil. Therefore do not be foolish, but understand what the Lord's will is.

EPHESIANS 5:15-17

The summer blockbuster is finally in theaters. After three years of production and postproduction, the opening night for the long-awaited guaranteed smash hit has arrived! The first viewing is completely packed. It was sold out just five minutes after the online ticket portal went live. The audience shuffles to their seats with sodas and popcorn in hand. A buttery aroma fills the air, along with the hushed whispers of excitement as the lights in the theater dim and the first preview begins to play.

After sitting through five movie previews for upcoming films, it's finally time for the feature presentation. An iconic studio logo and its familiar theme music play first. This is followed by an epic movie title that animates across the screen, and then the first chords of the movie soundtrack begin to play as the setting of the film is revealed. After a few set-up scenes,

the audience is introduced to the story's main character, and the early undertones of the conflict are established.

After two hours aboard a roller coaster of rising and falling tension, conflict, action, and key plot twists that take the audience by surprise, some flashback scenes and jaw-dropping reveals bring the summer epic to its peak. Viewers await only the impending monumental-scale battle sequence that brings the story to its hard-fought and necessary resolution.

But at that very moment, the movie shuts off. The house lights turn on, and the audience begins to exit their rows, hugging their empty popcorn buckets and half-consumed soda cups as they head for the door. There's no applause. There's no confusion as to why the movie has stopped playing. The entire audience behaves as if this is normal. They make their way to their cars, and head home.

Without any explanation or discussion about what I just described, you know full well that would never happen. That fictitious account is so foreign to our sensibilities as storytellers, as movie-goers, as humans. Animals do not contemplate great stories, but we do. We are God's image bearers, and as such, we gravitate to a good story because God is the master Storyteller and we are in his grand story.

Watch the Entire Movie

As silly and unnatural as that pretend movie story is, I share it for this reason. There is a decades-long trend in the church at large of telling only part of the story, and leaving out the ending. As the church, we have shown people three-quarters of the movie and had them walk out before the ending. Oh, we know the good guys win, but we miss the heart-pounding action and key details of the end of the story.

When the church fails to encounter the end of the story, it leaves people anemic and without the depth they need to get through the instability of our times with their faith and sanity intact. For various reasons (some quite understandable), most churches rarely (if ever) teach anything in depth related to eschatology (the study of last things).

Yet at the same time, most of these same churches would agree that the principle of casting vision for the future is a key factor in effective leadership for the church. Every good coach knows that they need to establish end-of-season goals for their team, and these goals serve to drive passion and guide decisions for the entire season.

Every business leader knows you must cast a clear vision for a company so everyone knows where the goal line is. Doing this effectively provides a single point of focus for everyone on the team. It inspires passion. It motivates progress. Most of all, it provides hope and direction.

When the church stops pointing people to their prophesied future, this essential vision casting is lost. The church of late tends to only look back. Looking back to the work of the cross and the victory of the resurrection is essential, to be sure. But without the critical focus on our amazing future present as well, believers are left with only the basics and have no real vision of the future to live in light of.

Christians must be a people of both reflection and anticipation. We reflect on what Christ has done to secure our salvation, and we anticipate his return and all the amazing events related to it and surrounding it. We cannot divorce heaven from the related events that lead us there!

My friends, may we never forget that we have an empty tomb to look back on, an occupied throne to look up to, and an amazing future to look forward to. Our salvation was secured in the first century, and prophesied long before that. The times in which we live are under the authority and sovereignty of God, who is always on the throne. And our future will consist of the final glorious phases of everything, including our very salvation.

We have been saved from the penalty of our sins. We are being saved from the power of sin. And one day, we will be saved from the very presence of sin. Our salvation is not complete. It is guaranteed, but not yet finished. The church at large tends to point people only to the down payment for believers' salvation and it often avoids to point people to the future culmination of salvation.

Dietrich Bonhoeffer, a German Lutheran pastor who courageously stood up to Hitler and lost his life as the consequence, wrote, "The Church of Christ bears witness to the end of all things. It lives from the end, it thinks from the end, it acts from the end, it proclaims its message from the end."[13] Unless the body of Christ has a clear, truthful, and compelling vision of the end, we are missing a key driving force that guides us toward our destiny with a sense of confidence, hope, joy, and tenacity.

Serving *from* the Future

With the end in mind, everything changes. When we as Christians live with a biblical vision of our future, it gives new life to our calling, new depth to our ministry, new urgency in our witness, new steel in our resolve, new strength in our godliness, and new fire in our purpose. Remembering that we are citizens of heaven and that our bema seat rewards will reverberate throughout eternity helps us put our present-day struggles into their proper perspective.

In light of all of our future blessing, I want to challenge you to reevaluate your calling and sense of purpose. I invite you to take some time to pray about what the Lord may lead you to do as a result. He calls us to higher ground. He calls us to things that make an eternal impact. He calls us to leverage everything we have and everything we are to extend his rule and glorify his name.

So do not walk out of the theater before the end of the story. Make a commitment to grapple with the truths of Bible prophecy, eschatology, and the incredible details about our future in heaven. Living from the future in this way will make today more focused, purposeful, hopeful, and joyful.

The verse at the beginning of this chapter bears repeating: "Be very careful, then, how you live—not as unwise but as wise, making the most of every opportunity, because the days are evil. Therefore do not be foolish, but understand what the Lord's will is" (Ephesians 5:15-17).

CHAPTER 17

Inviting Others to Join Us in Heaven

I, when I am lifted up from the earth, will draw all people to myself.

JOHN 12:32

I grew up inside the DC beltway, in a sprawl-and-crawl suburban setting. But once every year, I would get the opportunity to visit my grandmother and my uncles who ran a dairy farm in the Catskill Mountains of upstate New York. Situated across the way from my grandmother's house was a cornfield and a fairly shallow river. Behind her house were a couple of barns, a line of old apple trees, and acres upon acres of hay fields. Quite a contrast to the DC-metropolitan area.

When we would visit there as children, my sister and I would reconnect with local friends and play hide-and-seek for hours. We would build forts out of the hay bales in the barn—much to my uncles' frustration. We would catch frogs in the ponds and hunt for crayfish in the river. For a kid from suburbia, this place was like heaven on earth.

After each trip, I would return to the city and tell my stepbrother about this wonderful setting and the adventures that were had there. He and I are the same age, and we have enjoyed a built-in friendship since the first grade. Finally, one summer he joined us for the trip, and I was so excited that he could get to experience what I had been telling him about for the last several years.

When you care about someone, you want to involve them in the good things you have the blessing of taking part in. You invite them to join with you in your experience. You can't help but to share the good things in your life with them. This should be our mindset as we invite others to experience heaven with us.

Considering all that we have discussed in this book, my prayer is that we develop a deep passion and an urgency to share the good news of the gospel with others so we can join with as many other people as possible as residents of heaven. Ultimately, God must draw people and they must respond. We can't save anyone, only the Holy Spirit can. But incredibly, God uses our witness to draw people in and call them into a relationship with Christ. We should hope that our excitement for heaven is contagious to others as we naturally go about sharing what we love.

So this chapter serves as a call for readers. A call to creative, effective, and relevant evangelism. There is no cookie-cutter way to point people to Christ, but perhaps, with a little intentionality, boldness, and passion, you and I can help people to see the attractiveness of a relationship with Christ and the beauty of heaven.

Below are four practical suggestions that I would encourage you to pray through as you respond to whatever the Holy Spirit is leading you to do as a result of studying the topic of heaven with me. You see, that is the beauty of Bible study. When we study God's Word as believers in Christ, the Holy Spirit uses it to effect change and call us to action. He stirs within our spirit as he guides and directs us. God loves us too much to leave us where we are at, so he is always calling us toward our next steps of obedience and growth.

Like every good parent, our heavenly Father knows we will have wanted to do more when we get to the end of our time here on earth. He does not desire for us to have that *Schindler's List* moment I described in chapter 5, where we wish we would have done more about the things in life that really count.

As the church in the West continues its prophesied drift from her moorings, it is all the more reason why remnant believers must keep preaching the truth, pointing people to the Savior, and talking about the glory of heaven that awaits those who put their trust in Jesus Christ. Here are the four practical steps you can prayerfully consider.

Four Practical Steps

Practical Step #1: Pray for Opportunities to Share Your Faith

You may be surprised to find that if you pray for something that aligns with God's will, you just might get it. Paul tells us,

> The Spirit helps us in our weakness. We do not know what we ought to pray for, but the Spirit himself intercedes for us through wordless groans. And he who searches our hearts knows the mind of the Spirit, because the Spirit intercedes for God's people in accordance with the will of God (Romans 8:26-27).

If you sincerely pray that God would put people in your path who need to hear the gospel, and you remain open and alert to the leading of the Holy Spirit, the Lord will provide opportunities for you to share your faith with others. This could be someone at the coffee shop, a person in the checkout line at the grocery store, a close friend at school, or a fellow parent who waits in the pickup line at our kids' school.

Practical Step #2: Pray for Boldness

Even while we seek to avoid being pushy with our faith and always be sensitive to the response of others as we dialogue with them about the Lord, these things should not keep us from praying for boldness. When we have established trust and mutual respect with others, and find ourselves in the midst of those opportunities when a discussion has led to talking about the deeper things related to the brokenness of our world—separation from God, sin, salvation, and the like—we must boldly proclaim truth. Peter exhorts us:

> In your hearts revere Christ as Lord. Always be prepared to give an answer to everyone who asks you to give the reason for the hope that you have. But do this with gentleness and respect (1 Peter 3:15).

Practical Step #3: Set Some Goals

Why is it we set goals for so many things in our life, but somehow, when it comes to spiritual matters like praying to God, studying the Bible, or sharing our faith, we tend to think that it is not spiritual to do so? People often say they would rather wait on the leading of the Holy Spirit. Perhaps that is a cop out, putting all the impetus on the Lord instead of taking initiative ourselves.

The thing about goals is that we will never reach any goal that we do not set. Granted, we may not achieve every goal we make, but one thing is certain: 100 percent of goals that are *not* set are never reached.

I am not proposing that we turn witnessing opportunities into checkboxes. That can lead to legalism. But what I am proposing is that we can prayerfully set a goal to witness to a certain number of people each week or each month or each year. Regardless of how many people we actually shared with at the end of the timeline, somehow, simply having a target sets our wheels in motion and makes our commitment to share our faith that much more concrete.

Practical Step #4: Just Tell Your Story

Many people are intimidated by the thought of explaining the gospel to others or journeying with someone step by step through the process of coming to saving faith in Jesus. When the opportunity arises, perhaps you can just briefly tell your own story of faith. You will need to gauge how much time you have and how deep into your story you want to go, but if you just share with another person the difference that Christ has made in your life, that could be enough to earn their interest and keep the conversation going.

Your Role

It is not your job to save anyone. Your job is to lift Jesus up. Your job is to be a witness. A witness merely shares what they saw happen. Nothing more, nothing less. That alleviates the pressure that we place onto ourselves, and allows us to tell others simply and honestly about the change that the Lord has made in our lives. You just might find out that some specific detail that you shared as part of your story was exactly the thing a person needed to hear.

In this chapter, we have addressed our outward response to what we have been learning about heaven. But what becomes our inward response? How can this study impact us personally? Well, that is exactly what we are going to look at in the final chapter of this book.

Living in Anticipation of Heaven

*Our light and momentary troubles
are achieving for us an eternal glory
that far outweighs them all. So we fix
our eyes not on what is seen, but on
what is unseen, since what is seen is
temporary, but what is unseen is eternal.*

2 CORINTHIANS 4:17-18

I never served in the military, but several of my friends and family members did. I remember them going to basic training (aka boot camp), where they would have little to no communication with those on the outside, and where their personal world got turned completely upside down.

In boot camp, the aim is to take young civilians—some of whom are already fairly disciplined, and others who certainly are not—and turn them into battle-ready soldiers in a relatively brief period of time. Depending on the branch of service and some other details, boot camp typically will run between

6–13 weeks, and it will involve intense military training, preparing cadets for several years of work or a full career of serving in the military.

We're Just Getting Started!

Similarly, our short few decades of life on this tiny ball of dust and water we call planet Earth are merely getting us ready for the real adventure. It is boot camp for eternity. What we do now reverberates forever, so there is much at stake as we complete our training.

We need to live by embodying what has been coined as a *dash* mentality. Every tombstone in a graveyard lists two dates, with a dash in the middle. We don't control either of the dates, but we have great influence on how we handle the dash. If we approach our life with an eternal mindset—with our eyes fixed on heaven—we will make the most of the dash.

As you focus on your dash with eyes toward heaven, be sure to regularly contemplate all of the milestones believers have in store for them ahead. These are worth keeping our sights on as we navigate boot camp and will help to see us through.

To recap, here is a condensed, basic order of events that are the promised future for a believer in Christ (with a few additional details provided to complete the picture). As you read through these brief descriptions, please do so with the understanding and intentional acceptance that you will literally experience each of these personally!

FINAL KEY EVENTS

- Battle of Armageddon/defeat of the nations
- Beast and false prophet thrown into lake of fire
- Earth renovated/God's people ruling with him

- Satan released for last battle
- Satan thrown into lake of fire
- Great white throne judgment
- New heavens/new earth
- New Jerusalem

CHURCH AGE	TRIBULATION	MILLENNIAL KINGDOM	ETERNAL STATE

ORDER OF EVENTS

EVENTS ON EARTH

Rapture

Antichrist rises out of a 10-ruler alliance

Antichrist takes the place of 3 of them

Antichrist confirms a covenant with Israel and many (officially starting the tribulation period)

Possible timing of the Ezekiel 38 War

Antichrist revealed/seal judgments begin

Trumpet judgments

Mid-trib events

Bowl judgments

Christ returns/Jewish people saved

Antichrist's armies defeated

Sheep and goat judgment

Old Testament saints resurrected

Millennial kingdom begins

One final rebellion

Satan cast into lake of fire

Great white throne judgment

New heavens/new earth created

Eternal state

EVENTS IN HEAVEN

Bema seat

Marriage

Church-age believers return with Christ

The Rapture

The rapture is a signless, imminent (could happen at any moment), and future event when all believers will be transformed and raised instantly to meet Jesus in the air, and then taken into heaven (John 14:2-3; 1 Corinthians 15:51-52; 1 Thessalonians 4:15-17). The dead in Christ will be resurrected first, then we who are still alive will be instantly changed and caught up with them in the air to meet the Lord. This will be an amazing reunion with believers who went before us and all other believers from the entire church age. This sudden, supernatural, and global event will set all the other key events into motion.

The Judgment Seat of Christ

The judgment seat of Christ, also known as the bema seat, is where we as church-age believers will receive an evaluation of our work for Christ after our salvation. It is where we will receive eternal rewards for use in the kingdom and beyond. Various crowns are mentioned, and other rewards include varying levels of responsibility as we rule and reign with Christ.

The Marriage

The mystical union of Christ and the church will be formalized. Our longing to be with Christ and his longing to be with the church will finally be an official and permanent reality. This will all happen with much fanfare and celebration.

Meanwhile on earth…

Gap Period

We learn in 2 Thessalonians 2:7-8 that the restrainer (the Holy Spirit indwelling church-age believers) must first be taken out of the way (via the rapture) before the man of sin (the antichrist) can be revealed. Daniel 9 informs us that the tribulation period (i.e., Daniel's "seventieth week") formally begins when an agreement with the "many" is finalized by the antichrist (Daniel 9:27). Because the context of Daniel 9 concerns Israel, it makes sense that this agreement that will be brokered by the antichrist will be between Israel and the "many." Logic demands a presumably short gap of time before the tribulation begins.

Ezekiel 38 War

This prophecy foretells of a specific end-times attack against Israel that will come from the north. There is a lot of evidence to indicate that this will be a post-rapture power grab led by Russia, in partnership with Iran, Turkey, and others (see Ezekiel 38–39). Experts vary on where this war fits into the end-times order of events, but I think it will occur just before or soon after the tribulation period begins.

The Tribulation Period

In the chaotic aftermath of the rapture, a world leader will rise to power and broker a deal between Israel and "many," officially beginning the seven-year tribulation period. The antichrist will break his covenant with Israel exactly at the midpoint of the seven-year period and defile the temple (Daniel 9:27), and turn against the Jewish people (Revelation 12:13). A remnant of the Jewish people will be protected and will turn to Christ as Savior at the end of the tribulation period (Daniel 12:1-2; Matthew 23:39; Romans 11:25-27; Revelation 12:13-17; 14:1-5).

Now, back to your regularly scheduled program in heaven…

The Return of Christ to Earth

At the end of the tribulation period, Jesus will physically return to earth's surface accompanied by the armies of heaven (angels and church-age believers) who are following behind him (Revelation 19:11-18). The beast (antichrist) and the false prophet will be thrown into the lake of fire, and all their armies will be annihilated (Revelation 19:19-21).

[75-DAY] INTERVAL

The 75-Day Transition

The book of Daniel indicates a mysterious 75-day period between Christ's return and the beginning of the millennial kingdom (Daniel 12:11-12). Likely, this is when everything that needs to take place in order to establish the millennial kingdom will occur. This could include the cleanup from the destruction of the armies of the antichrist, the renovation of the earth, and the wedding supper of the Lamb (scholars vary on where they place this latter event).

The Millennial Kingdom

The Old Testament contains many prophecies of a yet-future golden era when a descendant of David will rule the entire world from Jerusalem. This 1,000-year period (Revelation 20:1-6) will follow the tribulation and the 75-day interval. Church-age believers will rule and reign with Christ, making his name known across the earth. At the end of this time, Satan will be released for one final deception and battle. He will quickly be defeated, and then thrown into the lake of fire, where he will remain permanently (Revelation 20:7-10).

The Great White Throne Judgment

At this judgment, all the nonbelievers from throughout history will stand before God to be judged, and sadly, cast into the lake of fire. Believers will not stand before God at this judgment because their sins have been covered by the atonement of Jesus (Revelation 20:11-15). Likely, believers will be residing in their custom-built living spaces in the new Jerusalem during this judgment, and also during the final event on our timeline.

The New Heaven and New Earth

All of creation will be completely renovated or recreated. Everything will be restored! The center of activity and God's presence will be in the new Jerusalem, but we will presumably be able to spend eternity traveling the vast expanse of heaven.

Comfort One Another

There is one point that I have not yet addressed in this book that I wanted to make sure I leveraged for those who may be reading this book as they grieve a loved one who recently died, or try to cope with tremendous losses from years gone by. I want to make sure that you find answers to your questions about heaven. Also, I want to do my best to give you some comfort and encouragement in the midst of your grief. Death is not the end.

One fact Paul addressed in his first letter to the church in Thessalonica—a church that he planted and spent only three weeks discipling—was their concern for loved ones who were believers and who had died. Their church community was suffering persecution, and some believers were martyred. Paul had taught them the basics of eschatology, yet they were confused because they thought that the Lord would return in their lifetime.

Paul addressed their concerns in 1 Thessalonians 4:13-18. There, we find Paul's main teaching on the doctrine of the rapture, and he ended the extensive play-by-play description with a compelling and telling expression. We've read a few of these verses throughout our study, but I wanted to share the larger context surrounding why Paul was addressing this subject in the first place. We witness Paul's heartfelt and encouraging care for the body of Christ in this section of Scripture. Here's what we read in that passage:

> Brothers and sisters, we do not want you to be uninformed about those who sleep in death, so that you do not grieve like the rest of

mankind, who have no hope. For we believe that Jesus died and rose again, and so we believe that God will bring with Jesus those who have fallen asleep in him. According to the Lord's word, we tell you that we who are still alive, who are left until the coming of the Lord, will certainly not precede those who have fallen asleep. For the Lord himself will come down from heaven, with a loud command, with the voice of the archangel and with the trumpet call of God, and the dead in Christ will rise first. After that, we who are still alive and are left will be caught up together with them in the clouds to meet the Lord in the air. And so we will be with the Lord forever. Therefore encourage one another with these words.

There are two phrases I want to highlight. First, in verse 13, Paul points out that as believers we "do not grieve like the rest of mankind, who have no hope." It is not that we do not grieve. I have lost some who were close to me. I grieved because it is not natural. Death is not supposed to be. But the key point to note here is that we do not grieve as the world grieves. The world possesses no hope for their future, no concept of a sovereign God who has all things under his loving guidance toward a good, ultimate, and righteous conclusion.

Christ followers, on the other hand, have hope. Our hope is in the next life. And it is a guaranteed hope that will be greater than anything we can even imagine.

The second phrase I want to highlight is in Paul's conclusion on the topic. In verse 18, he explains the intended use for the doctrine of the rapture, where he wrote, "Therefore encourage one another with these words."

The promise of the resurrection and the anticipation for the rapture should cause every believer to be uplifted, as we await a wonderful reunion where we get to rejoin believers who have gone before us—all in the presence of the Savior who makes it all possible. Therefore, encourage one another with these words!

And I know that the reality exists that you may have had nonbelieving loved ones who have died. We entrust them into the Lord's hands and must strive to relinquish that to the Lord by faith. Who knows, we may be surprised that some of them actually made a decision for Christ before they died. For the rest, we trust that our God always does what is best. He alone is holy and perfect.

Thankfully, we are promised in clear terms that for those of us who have experienced loss and pain "'he will wipe every tear from their eyes. There will be no more death' or mourning or crying or pain, for the old order of things has passed away" (Revelation 21:4).

The Best Is Yet to Come

In the introduction to this book, I shared the first two verses from Colossians 3, but I didn't unpack them. There, I wanted to simply set the stage for the book, and now that we are at the end, I want to return full circle back to those verses. In its wider context, Colossians 3:1-4 reads,

> Since, then, you have been raised with Christ, set your hearts on things above, where Christ is, seated at the right hand of God. Set your minds on things above, not on earthly things. For you died, and your life is now hidden with Christ in God. When Christ, who is your life, appears, then you also will appear with him in glory.

As believers, we have been made alive, but we often live as though we are still dead. When this passage says to "set your hearts," that is a rendering of the Greek word *zēteite* (from the root *zēteō*), and it means to seek with the intent of finding, to search, to demand (in some contexts), or to seek by inquiring. This is a verb—an action word. It is something we must be intentional about. In addition, when the passage refers to the object of that doing, "the things above," the term translated "above" is the Greek word *anō*, which means up or above, or more specifically here, the heavenly region or upward.

We gain meaningful insight when we look deeply into these verses, for we discover that there is a real cause-and-effect relationship that is present. There is something that impacts our gaze, and that thing is the fact that in Christ, we are raised from death to life. It is the cause. The effect of this amazing transaction is that we would naturally focus more on heavenly matters than on earthly matters. The key reason for all of this is that Christ (in whom we now possess new life) is seated in the honored position on the throne of heaven. The One you are united to is sovereign. God is running the show, and he has told us where all this life is headed.

When we face circumstances of struggle and stress in this life, we need to remind ourselves that this is not our home. This is not the end of our story. In fact, it is only the beginning. The best is yet to come! Our sovereign co-heir is on the throne, so we need not worry. We simply need to look up. We must live life standing on our tiptoes, locking our gaze on heaven as we anticipate the glories that we will one day experience.

Our affections follow our focus. Where we gaze determines our point of view. If our focus is constantly on our struggles, our hearts will feel defeated. But if our focus is on the realities of heaven and our future glory, our hearts will be full of joy. Joy and despair cannot occupy the same space at the same time. Neither can hope and hopelessness. The struggles of this life are very real but so are the realities of heaven.

The single most practical thing we can do as believers is to set our minds on the realities of heaven and our promised future. This puts wind in our sails, hope in our hearts, fire in our evangelism, steadfastness in our commitments, and a healthy longing for our true home in our hearts.

Christians are a people of reflection and anticipation. We reflect on what Christ has done and we anticipate what he is going to do. As I often say (and did so a few times earlier in this book), we have an empty tomb to look back on, an occupied throne to look up to, and an amazing future to look forward to. If we keep those three things in the front of our minds, we become unshakable. Isaiah 26:3 reads, "You will keep him in perfect peace, whose mind is stayed on You, because he trusts in You" (NKJV).

One day soon—by rapture or death—you (if you are a believer in Christ) and I will see our risen and glorified Lord face to face. We will be changed and have bodies fit for heaven. In the same way small seeds become giant trees and ground-bound caterpillars become air-gliding butterflies, you and I will receive bodies, minds, emotions, and abilities of which we cannot currently conceive. As we await this by faith, we can withstand anything the world, the flesh, or the devil throws at us.

So, stay strong as you walk through this life with your chin tilted toward heaven. The winds will blow. The waves will come. But we are anchored to heaven by an unbreakable tether. The best is truly yet to come!

In the words of John, found in the last two verses of the Bible, "He who testifies to these things says, 'Yes, I am coming soon.' Amen. Come, Lord Jesus. The grace of the Lord Jesus be with God's people. Amen."

1. Randy Alcorn, *Heaven* (Wheaton, IL: Tyndale, 2004), 7.

2. "The Global Religious Landscape," *Pew Research Center* (December 18, 2012), at https://www.pewre search.org/religion/2012/12/18/global-religious-landscape-exec/.

3. "Few Americans Blame God or Say Faith Has Been Shaken Amid Pandemic, Other Tragedies—2: Views on the Afterlife," *Pew Research Center* (November 23, 2021), at https://www.pewresearch.org/religion/2021/11/23/views-on-the-afterlife/.

4. Jeff Kinley, *Wake the Bride* (Eugene, OR: Harvest House, 2015), 85.

5. Blair Donovan and Tess Petak, "The 20 Most Expensive Celebrity Wedding Dresses of All Time," *Brides* (November 2, 2022), at https://www.brides.com/story/the-most-expensive-wedding-dresses-of-all-time.

6. Thomas L. Constable, *Notes on Revelation Commentary* (2022 edition), 300, at https://planobiblecha pel.org/tcon/notes/pdf/revelation.pdf.

7. Ed Hindson, *Future Glory* (Eugene, OR: Harvest House, 2021), 93.

8. Ron Rhodes, *The End Times in Chronological Order* (Eugene, OR: Harvest House, 2012), 72.

9. Nick Dellis, "1966 Shelby Production Numbers," *Mustang Specs*, at https://www.mustangspecs .com/1966-shelby-production-numbers/.

10. This section and the next is adapted material from *The Non-Prophet's Guide™ to the Book of Revelation*, pages 192-198.

11. Calculations taken from *The Revelation Record* by Dr. Henry Morris (Carol Stream, IL: Tyndale, 1983), 450-451.

12. C.S. Lewis, *The Problem of Pain* (New York: HarperCollins, 1940), 119-120.

13. Dietrich Bonhoeffer, *Creation and Fall; Temptation: Two Biblical Studies*, trans. John C. Fletcher; Kathleen Downham (New York: Simon and Schuster, 1997), 9.

Other Great Reading by Todd Hampson

The Non-Prophet's Guide™ to the End Times

Do you tend to avoid studying books of the Bible like Revelation and Ezekiel? Does it feel like words such as *rapture* and *apocalypse* fly right over your head? It's common to dismiss these and other topics related to Bible prophecy as irrelevant and…well…too complicated.

But God's Word says, "Blessed is the one who reads aloud the words of this prophecy, and blessed are those who hear it and take to heart what is written in it, because the time is near" (Revelation 1:3).

Prepare to be blessed in a meaningful way! *The Non-Prophet's Guide™ to the End Times* combines engaging illustrations with down-to-earth explanations to help you navigate the ins and outs of Bible prophecy. There's no better time to grasp God's plans for the future—and for you—than this very moment.

The Non-Prophet's Guide™ to the End Times Workbook

Dig deeper into what the Bible says about the end times and gain insight into God's plan for your future. Todd Hampson's companion workbook to his best-selling *The Non-Prophet's Guide™ to the End Times* makes the challenging study of Bible prophecy clear, understandable, and fun.

With more than 100 helpful and humorous graphics and illustrations, you can explore scriptural prophecies and discover answers for your questions about the last days, such as…

- How does fulfilled Bible prophecy affect our view of prophecies not yet fulfilled?
- What can we learn from those who were watching at Jesus' first coming?
- How can we discern between conspiracy theories and trustworthy facts that line up with end-time geopolitical signs?

The Non-Prophet's Guide™ to the Book of Revelation

If the final book of the Bible has ever left you scratching your head or wondering what to make of plagues and horsemen, your friendly Non-Prophet is here to help you read Revelation as never before.

Full of engaging graphics, author and illustrator Todd Hampson has created a user-friendly guide to John's prophecies about the last days. This concise and appealing study

- removes the fear factor and demystifies the capstone book of the Bible
- provides biblical clarity about the key events in the end-times
- helps reclaim your hope, confidence, and joy in the promised future

The Non-Prophet's Guide™ to the Book of Revelation offers informative study tools for understanding its prophecies, and practical challenges to apply God's truths to your life today.

The Non-Prophet's Guide™ to Spiritual Warfare

Even as a Christian, it can be difficult to discern the facts about the supernatural nature of good and evil. How much has pop culture influenced our ideas about angels and demons? Why do we as Christians face spiritual warfare when the Holy Spirit dwells within us? What limits exist on Satan's powers?

In *The Non-Prophet's Guide™ to Spiritual Warfare*, bestselling author and illustrator Todd Hampson gets to the heart of your questions about spiritual battles, angels, demons, the nature of evil, and more. With Todd's signature combination of light-hearted illustrations and thoughtful applications of Scripture, this guide is both easy to understand and deeply informative.

You will learn to…

- discern between cultural myths and biblical facts about the supernatural
- recognize the real threats you face while remaining grounded in God's truth
- understand why being ready to stand against demonic influence is more important now than ever before

The Non-Prophet's Guide™ to Spiritual Warfare will give you the resources you need to champion spiritual battles, while inspiring you to dive deeper into God's Word to equip yourself with truth.

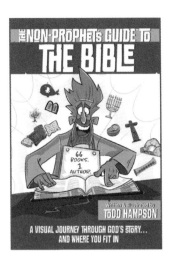

The Non-Prophet's Guide™ to the Bible

The world's all-time bestseller, the Bible, is truly unique: an ancient collection of 66 separate books written across 1,500 years that fits together like a perfectly crafted puzzle. It proclaims itself to be the Word of God—and supports this claim with hundreds of specific, now-fulfilled prophecies.

Because of its massive cultural impact, readers of all backgrounds and beliefs ask questions about the Bible's context, history, purpose, and reliability. Enter *The Non-Prophet's Guide™ to the Bible*: a bright, infographic-packed panorama designed to give you

- a section-by-section overview of the Bible, illuminating each book's distinct role in telling God's story
- a crash course on who wrote the Scriptures, when they were written, and how they were preserved through the ages
- the compelling case for why you can believe the Bible truly is the Word of God

Whether you're a longtime believer looking to better understand Scripture or an interested newcomer seeking answers about Christianity, this accessible guide provides the insight and information you need to see how the Bible portrays a global history that has unfolded in the direction of God's promises.

The Chronological Guide to Bible Prophecy

This fun and informative book provides a comprehensive survey of the many prophecies found in Scripture, underlining their themes and illuminating why they bring us hope today. This resource will deepen your sense of wonder for the Bible's accuracy, while guiding you through a timeline of God's pledges to his people. You will...

- examine completed Bible prophecies—and witness how these unbroken promises create clear and compelling apologetics for your faith

- understand the prophesied events that are still to come and the order in which they will occur

- grow in reverence for our incredible God, who uses prophecy to make his amazing faithfulness known to us

The Non-Prophet's Guide™ to the Book of Daniel

In today's increasingly unstable culture, we need the wealth of wisdom available in the book of Daniel, which teaches us to live boldly and joyfully for the Lord, even in the most difficult circumstances.

Through Daniel, you'll discover what it means to stand for righteousness in a world filled with compromise. And you'll learn how to do so *winsomely*, in a way that both enables others to gain a clear understanding of who God is and compels them to seek after him.

Explore the many vivid prophecies Daniel had about the days to come—prophecies that shed much light on what will happen during the end times and are deeply practical for our day. You will find your faith strengthened as you see the many ways that God has kept his promises and will continue to do so.

God used Daniel's faithfulness and courage powerfully in his day, and he can do the same through our lives today as we apply the lessons meant to help us fulfill our role in God's divine story right now.

To learn more about our Harvest Prophecy resources, please visit:

www.HarvestProphecyHQ.com

HARVEST PROPHECY
An Imprint of Harvest House Publishers